I0030955

Contracting, Logistics, Reverse Logistics:
The Project, Program and Portfolio Approach

CONTRACTING, LOGISTICS, REVERSE LOGISTICS

The Project, Program and Portfolio Approach

Dr. Robert Lee Gordon

Westphalia Press
An Imprint of the Policy Studies Organization
Washington, DC
2016

CONTRACTING, LOGISTICS, REVERSE LOGISTICS
All Rights Reserved © 2016 by Policy Studies Organization

Westphalia Press
An imprint of Policy Studies Organization
1527 New Hampshire Ave., NW
Washington, D.C. 20036
info@ipsonet.org

ISBN-10: 1-63391-406-2
ISBN-13: 978-1-63391-406-3

Cover and interior design by Jeffrey Barnes
jbarnesbook.design

Daniel Gutierrez-Sandoval, Executive Director
PSO and Westphalia Press

Updated material and comments on this edition
can be found at the Westphalia Press website:
www.westphaliapress.org

Acknowledgements

The author would like to recognize and acknowledge the contributions of Dr. Wanda Curlee, who assisted in the research and completion of this book. Dr. Wanda Curlee and I have collaborated on several books, and dozens of articles and in many ways this book would not have been as complete without her input and feedback. Her diligence, ideas, and assistance have led to the completion of this text.

Dedication

This book is dedicated to my wife, Linda Gordon, whose support throughout the years has sustained our happiness. With her support, we have raised two wonderful children who are moving forward with their academic careers as well as raising multiple animals along the way.

SECTION ONE
HISTORICAL PERSPECTIVES

CHAPTER ONE
INTRODUCTION

Contracting, logistics, and reverse logistics are intertwined with the project management discipline. In recent years, the project management institute has expanded certifications into the strategic areas of program and portfolios. Contracting, logistics, and reverse logistics depending on the industry are strategic opportunities. American Public University System (APUS) offers degrees in government contracting, transportation and logistics, and reverse logistics. All three programs benefit from an overlapping text that demonstrates how project, program, and portfolio management (PPPM) drives better strategy. Ultimately, successful strategy leads to increased value and the difficult topics of ethics, culture, relationships, and a company's return on investment (ROI).

Undergraduate students with a primary focus toward government contracting and acquisition, transportation and logistics, and reverse logistics are the beneficiaries of this text. The workbooks assist the student to understand the interconnection between the project management discipline and the student's area of focus.

The text delivers the same knowledge to a student in one major while taking electives in one of the other majors. For example, the student majoring in transportation and logistics taking an elective in reverse logistics and/or government contracting and acquisition would benefit by having the same andragogy delivered.

The book is divided into 9 sections and a total of 28 chapters. Each section culminates with a summary of each section. The textbook is followed by three workbooks: one each for contracting, logistics, and reverse logistics. The workbooks provide case studies, questions, and essays for each case study, while chapters are concluded with proposed weekly discussion questions, sample test/quiz questions for each chapter. These chapter questions could be used to populate potential final exams.

Section One

- Chapter 2 provides the history of project management and the newer identified strategic areas of program and portfolio management.

- Chapter 3 presents a history of U.S. government contracting and acquisition.

- Chapter 4 reviews the history of transportation and logistics.

- Chapter 5 offers the history of the newest area reverse logistics.

- Chapter 6 concludes the section with a summary of the previous five chapters.

Section Two

- Chapter 7 presents the inter-relationship of project management and contracting and acquisition.

- Chapter 8 reviews the inter-relationship of project management and transportation and logistics.

- Chapter 9 offers the inter-relationship of project management and reverse logistics.

- Chapter 10 concludes the section with a summary of the previous three chapters.

Section Three

- Chapter 11 presents the inter-relationship of program management and contracting and acquisition.

- Chapter 12 reviews the inter-relationship of program management and transportation and logistics.

- Chapter 13 offers inter-relationship of program management and reverse logistics.

- Chapter 14 concludes the section with a summary of the previous three chapters.

Section Four

- Chapter 15 presents the inter-relationship of portfolio management and contracting and acquisition.

- Chapter 16 reviews the inter-relationship of portfolio management and transportation and logistics.

- Chapter 17 offers the inter-relationship of portfolio management and reverse logistics.

- Chapter 18 concludes the section with a summary of the previous three chapters.

Section Five

- Chapter 19 provides the ethics and culture in modern PPPM.

- Chapter 20 presents the ethics and culture in contracting and acquisition.

- Chapter 21 reviews the ethics and culture in transportation and logistics.

- Chapter 22 offers the ethics and culture in reverse logistics.

- Chapter 22 concludes the section with a summary of the previous four chapters.

Section Six

- Chapter 24 provides the future of modern PPPM.

- Chapter 25 presents the future of contracting and acquisition.

- Chapter 26 reviews the future of transportation and logistics.

- Chapter 26 offers the future of reverse logistics.

- Chapter 28 concludes the section with a summary of the previous four chapters.

Section Seven—Contracts workbook

Section Eight—Transportation and logistics workbook

Section Nine—Reverse logistics workbook

Section one has six chapters. Each chapter provides a history of the major areas of the book. Sections two, three, and four cover the inter-relationship between PPPM and the areas initially covered in chapters three, four, and five. Section five approaches the ethical aspects of each of the topics. Sections six discusses the future of PPPM; contracting and acquisition; transportation and logistics; and reverse logistics. Sections seven through nine are workbooks that pertain to each of the areas that offer case studies, and discussion and quiz questions. Through each of the topic areas, the reader will have a well-rounded understanding of the project management discipline, contracting and acquisition, transportation and logistics, and reverse logistics.

Integrated Supply Chain

As an introduction to the three areas that will be covered, there is a need to understand and explain an integrated supply chain. An integrated supply chain combines the disciplines of contract management, logistics, and reverse logistics to achieve greater results than one would achieve by keeping these functional areas in separate silos. Understandably, many organizations attempt to keep these areas separate for various reasons; however, not considering the system as connected would be making a serious mistake. Supply chains are understood to be series of systems and processes; however, all of those processes and systems need to share information during the various steps. When all steps are not integrated and connected, valuable information is lost resulting in incorrect assumptions regarding material needs. When systems do not share information, future demand will be incorrectly forecasted causing a ripple of issues within an organization. Firms that have integrated their supply chain functions have benefited from value enhancement for their supply chain management efforts (Wisner, Tan, & Leong, 2012).

When an organization is not integrating contracting, logistics and reverse logistics an organization will not be taking advantage of these changes to better address the entire supply chain. Supply chain management requires processes and exchanges that involve multiple organizations (Boyer & Verma, 2010). For example, if a supplier lacks consumption feedback, then the supplier might not be able to accurately predict demand. If returns are not taking into the equation, there might be the perception of an artificial demand that results in overstock or shortages. Incorrect forecasts results in additional costs for the organization as shortages results in unhappy customers or surpluses result in stock sitting for a long period, costing the company holding the inventory money due to costs of carrying inventory.

According to Blanchard (2010), a supply chain is unique to an organization and although there are similarities, using a one size fits all approach will not be successful. Every organization has a unique supply chain, and although there can be best practices for the industry, there needs to be policies and procedures that address the unique features of the organization's supply chain. In closing, if the processes are not developed to support the organization and the organization does not integrate contracts, logistics, and reverse logistics the organization will not have a successful supply chain.

Chapter One—Discussion/Quiz Questions

a. What is an integrated supply chain?

b. Why is an integrated supply chain important to contracts, logistics, and reverse logistics?

c. Is future demand predictable? Why or why not?

d. Do incorrect forecasts impact a supply chain?

e. Is a supply chain generic and transferable to any company or industry?

CHAPTER TWO
HISTORY OF MODERN PROJECT, PROGRAM AND PORTFOLIO MANAGEMENT

The Project Management discipline continues to evolve and is being affected by the rapid technology changes. The project management institute (PMI) has added several foundational standards to its original Guide to the Project Management Book of Knowledge, commonly referred to as the PMBOK Guide. For the purpose of this chapter, the other two foundational standards that will be reviewed will be the program standard and the portfolio standard. The most widely known project management certification is PMI's project management professional (PMP). The PMP was the first certification sponsored by PMI and was already prevalent in the early 1990s. The program management professional (PgMP) was introduced by PMI in 2007. In 2014, the portfolio management professional (PfMP) made its debut. Through the years, the PMI has realized that strategy has become a vital part of implementing changes within an organization, whether it is civilian or military.

Modern Project Management

Documentation of Ancient engineering and architectural feats may have included project management principles. The Bible provided a detailed account of King Solomon building the Temple and his palace (1 Kings 5:1–7:51, King James Version), which were built around 966 B.C. The details included a list of supplies, dimensions, description of the exterior and interior, where the provisions came from, and a listing of resources. Additionally, the order in which the construction took place was also listed. The timeframe to build the temple was 7 years, while the palace took 13 years. Solomon declared, "I purpose to build a house unto the name of the Lord my God" (1 Kings 5:5, King James Version). The temple was built to glorify and thank God (1 Kings 5:5, King James Version).

The Egyptians, before Solomon, built great architectural structures like the Pyramids. The Egyptian Pyramids date from 2686 to 2125 B.C. Haan (2014) described how the burial sites were constructed. The Egyptians appeared to have used some project management concepts, including the management of resources, scope and quality, and integration management (Haan, 2014). These structures were built as a burial site that would assist the deceased to transition to the afterlife, as is the belief of the ancient Egyptians (Haan, 2014).

There was also evidence of project management in the past East Asian cultures. Pheng and Lee (1997) provided comparisons of Zhuge Liang's book *Art of Management* and Western project management practices. Liang's book was written ~1,600 years ago in China. Liang was a Taoist. The Taoists believed that there was no absolute wrong or right. Pheng and Lee (1997) forwarded Liang's military concepts to project management concepts. Liang's thoughts about management included the following:

- Organizations had to be organized and managed.
- Organizations and war required strategies and tactics.
- The leadership of any army and organization had an important influence in shaping success.
- They both needed high quality and committed people.
- They both thrived on information (Pheng & Lee, 1997, p. 2).

The PMBOK (PMI, 2013a), as well as Backlund, Chronéer, and Sundqvist (2015), discussed the importance of the above-mentioned qualities being project necessities.

The Inca Empire, fifteen to sixteenth century A.D., exhibited project management skills in its road systems (Knapp, 2015; Schreffler, 2014). The road system was characterized by being very straight, even with major obstacles, and having several different types of buildings at junctures (Knapp, 2015; Schreffler, 2014). Some of the buildings were military, religious, or political in nature.

There was also evidence that lodging existed for those who traveled the Inca road system, and lodging was within a day's travel or less (Knapp, 2015; Schreffler, 2014). The speculation is that the road systems met a need of the Inca elite which was to meet communication and military needs (Knapp, 2015; Schreffler, 2014). One may extrapolate that the Inca Empire may have used relatively advanced engineering principles for the road systems that in turn would have required some aspects of project management. The Inca's project management may have included resource, integration, and milestone management, but not cost and schedule management.

Evidence of project management throughout the ages was documented by those in power. King Solomon, the Pharaohs, and the Inca Empire leaders were extremely wealthy and powerful (Haan, 2014; 1 Kings 5, King James Version; Knapp, 2015; Schreffler, 2014) and did not demonstrate concern for cost and schedule. The PMBOK (PMI, 2013a) states that a project assisted an organization to realize its business approach which normally includes meeting organizational strategies and project goal achievement, including budgets and timeframes (Backlund et al., 2015). The pyramids, temples, and many buildings mentioned in the Bible were to glorify God or the person in charge of construction (Haan, 2014; 1 Kings 5, King James Version), with no regard to adhering to a schedule and budget.

These ancient projects' characteristics were different from modern project management. The PMBOK defined the work of project management as the following:

- Include competing demands for scope, time, cost, risk, and quality.
- Resolves stakeholders with differing needs and expectations.
- Specifies identified requirements (PMI, 2013a).

The ancient architectural and engineering feats did not appear to have to compete with differing demands in the areas of scope, time, cost, risk, or quality. Solomon and Pharaoh were all-powerful during the construction time, so they dictated the demands (Haan, 2014; 1 Kings 5). Also, the rulers were the stakeholders, and therefore, there were no "differing needs and expectations" (PMI, 2013a).

The beginnings of modern project management had been recognized as the late 1950s and early 1960s (Kwak & Anbari, 2012) with the development of the project evaluation and review technique (PERT). PERT, a critical path method (CPM), was developed for the Polaris submarine program. The project was so large that a computer-based system to track the development of the program had to be developed. The U.S. aerospace industry, the U.S. Department of Defense, and large U.S. construction companies drove the project management discipline during this era. The focus appeared to be on improving profitability while developing new technology (Kwak & Anbari, 2012).

Project management techniques such as PERT, CPM, and earned value management (EVM) were included in many computer tools, and most industries apply some forms of project management tools to their projects (Kwak & Anbari, 2012). Modern project management was defined as work on a project that competed for resources, scope, cost, and schedule (PMI, 2013a) and in addition, used modern metric techniques, such as PERT, CPM, and EVM (Kwak & Anbari, 2015; PMI, 2013a), and technology to enhance communication speed and methodology practice (Kwak & Anbari, 2012). Others, further defined project management to include planning, organizing, directing, and controlling events and company resources to achieve goals of the project's interested parties (Kwak & Anbari, 2012).

Depending on the company's culture, the project manager's role can be vastly different. In a company culture that promoted project management, there may be several levels of project managers. According to Backlund et al. (2015), benchmark of a best-in-class project management organization had four different positions with increasing responsibility and knowledge. The levels were differentiated by education, skill, experience, and other factors that a PMO should evaluate when classifying project management talent.

The project manager may be given overall authority to achieve project objectives or may be relegated to a role of monitoring tasks (Kerzner, 2014). Within these two extremes, the project manager needed to understand the functional and organizational structure of the company, how to negotiate within the structure, and how to overcome the lack of clearly defined authority (Kerzner, 2014). Also, within these two extremes, the quality of the project management leadership may range from excellent to extremely bad (Backlund et al., 2015).

Levin (2010) stated that with the global economy and technology, the successful project manager was a communicator and a negotiator. The studies demonstrated that the successful project manager of leading edge technology products was able to identify "influential advisors" (2001) and potential customers to advocate the need for the radical technology changes. Levin (2010) continued that formal authority was not as significant for the project manager and the project team to be successful. The influence of the project manager appeared to exist by people skills and being a team player.

Earned value (EV) has continued to be an important measurement and status tool for project managers, developed from the cost/schedule control systems criteria (C/SCSC). In 1967, the U.S. Department of Defense adopted C/SCSC. This system was intended to help control major research and development projects by integrating cost, schedule, and technical performance management (Kwak & Anbari, 2012). The U.S. military was spending millions of dollars on complex weapon systems, and at the end of a project phase had nothing of substance. In the early 1960s, it was realized that something had to change (Kwak & Anbari, 2012).

The U.S. Air Force established a set of 35 criteria that constituted an acceptable management system (Kwak & Anbari, 2012). The criteria evolved into the C/SCSC which became the EV system. EV continued to be an integral part of project management tools, and the concept was at the foundation of training for new project managers. EV continued to be a part of government regulations overseeing projects. The agencies that used EVM were the U.S. Department of Defense, NASA, the U.S. Postal Service, and the U.S. Department of Energy (Backlund et al., 2015; Kerzner, 2014). PMI included EV as the core means for understanding the status of the project (PMI, 2013a). Evidence exists that EV is not the best method to use for statusing projects. Evidence suggests that customer satisfaction, milestone tracking, tying deliverables to milestones, and critical path monitoring are just as effective as EV (Backlund et al., 2015).

Technology and globalization have altered the traditional project management environment. Technology has allowed many projects to shift away from the traditional office setting. Technology allows and even encourages businesses to conduct project management in a virtual environment (Backlund et al., 2015; Kerzner, 2014).

Studies indicate that project managers leading virtual project teams need to be comfortable with technology (Duarte & Synder, 2006). The project manager must be able to use the technology as a tool rather than letting the technology dictate his/her style. Many allow technology to drive how the business or project is established rather than viewing technology as a tool.

The project manager may also be responsible, as a leader, to ensure that the technology is supportive of the team dynamics. The project manager must be able to manipulate or work around the systems to improve dynamics within the virtual team environment.

The project management environment has evolved. Many project managers may report to a program manager or portfolio manager. These are the latest areas of the project management discipline that PMI has recognized as having a strategic component.

Modern Program Management

Program management is bringing several projects together to realize a better benefit than doing the projects individually (Näsholm & Blomquist, 2015; PMI, 2013b). A formal definition of programs did not occur until ~2006 by PMI. The PMI decided that programs were not large projects. Up until this time, most companies and industries either interchanged projects and programs or defined a program as a large project. PMI's definition of programs was revolutionary. In the mid-2000s and even into the second decade, finding scholarly articles, trade journal articles, or even books that used PMI's definition did not exist. Until there was more acceptance of PMI's *The Standard for Program Management* (PMI, 2013b), the new definition was not seen in print. Slowly, program management has been accepted in most industries.

Programs, as defined by PMI, have been in existence as long as projects. The Inca's road system and lodging, the temple built by Solomon, and even the Pyramids were programs. All of these endeavors were "a group of related projects…managed in a coordinated way to obtain benefits …" (PMI, 2013b). The benefit as defined by PMI as "an outcome of … products … that provide utility to the sponsoring organization as well as the program intended beneficiaries" (PMI, 2013b). The ancient programs were a set of related projects, such as building the roadways and lodging, the temple with artisans, architects, and masons, and the same with the pyramids. The difference was the benefit as the sponsoring organization and the program intended beneficiary was the same.

Most governments have done programs before PMI defining it. Governments built ships for many years, designed and constructed missiles, planes, submarines, and even sent people to space and the moon. The U.S. government lost sight of this once project management became popular and the PMP certification became popular. The leaders in the Department of Defense and NASA somehow lost the sense of the importance of a program. Designing space vehicles and sending humans into space, and designing and constructing an aircraft carrier, submarine, or aircraft became large projects. The leaders in program management lost the advantage.

Oil and gas and construction have embraced programs and are leaders. NASA has become a major advocate of PMI and embraced the tenets of program management. The Department of Defense places more credibility with the Defense Acquisition University (DAU). The DAU offers free of charge to military personnel, certifications at the project and program levels. Many military personnel rather take these certifications as they are free of charge and focus on government acquisitions.

Whether the certification was obtained from PMI or DAU, it is important to note that programs are gaining traction in the government. Both PMI and DAU recognize the need for programs to deliver a strategic goal to the organization. The strategy could be delivering a new helicopter or constructing a new oil rig. It is also recognized that program managers need to understand the principles of project management. Project portfolio managers or also known as portfolio managers deliver a strategy to the company/organization by ensuring the right projects and programs are done.

Modern Portfolio Management

PMI, in 2006, recognized portfolio management as a project management discipline (Levin & Wyzalek, 2015). Portfolio management has been performed by financial institutions for many years. As project management software started to mature in the 1970s and 1980s, astute organizations started selecting projects that delivered to the strategic goals. These organizations did not reveal what they were doing as they realized it was a competitive advantage. They soon found that the tools were not enough (Levin & Wyzalek, 2015).

The portfolio manager should assist corporations with driving the performance of the investment and the benefits realization of the portfolio (Levin & Wyzalek, 2015, p. 123; PMI, 2013b). A culture shift is needed by the corporation for the portfolio manager to meet the strategic goals. Processes and procedures need to be established that focus the attention on the company's strategy. Business unit leaders need to make sure that they support the portfolio manager (Korhonen, Laine, & Martinsuo, 2014; Levin & Wyzalek, 2015; Müller, Martinsuo, & Blomquist, 2008).

Achieving strategic goals need to be the driving force of companies and the government. The portfolio manager with the assistance of the strategic leaders (C-Suite; Business Unit Heads; Flag and Senior Officers; and Government executives) establishes criteria selection for the portfolio. The traditional methods of balanced scorecards and cost/benefit analysis are not sufficient for project selection. The portfolio manager needs to understand the resource demands and project intra-dependencies (Lin, 2015). The portfolio manager should constantly be evaluating the portfolio for the strategic benefit, or value weighed against project and program dependencies and the ensuing resource demands (Lerch & Spieth, 2013; Lin, 2015).

When evaluating the portfolio, Kornfeld and Kara (2011) found leadership many times falls into the following traps:

1. How to optimize the portfolio to meet the future vision?.

2. Generating the right mix of projects/programs and benefit value.

3. How to properly measure the portfolio outcomes?

These three items need to drive strategy execution. According to Kornfeld and Kara (2011), strategy execution translated strategic objectives into portfolios to meet the strategic intent. Because organizations and governments have limited funds, not all projects and programs can be done. The portfolio manager recommends the portfolio mix to a governance board (Levin & Wyzalek, 2015; PMI, 2013c). The portfolio is monitored, projects and programs may be accelerated, delayed, canceled, or new ones added. As the portfolio shifts, the portfolio manager juggles the resources and the value realized (Kornfeld & Kara, 2011; PMI, 2013c). Lerch and Spieth (2013) advocated balancing the mix of projects and programs. The mix may be based on risk, project type (Research and Development versus implementation), or product development.

The PMI Thought Leadership Series Report (2015a) found that those organizations with a high portfolio management maturity met strategic objectives 71% of the time. In contrast, organizations with a low maturity met strategic goals 43% of the time. The study continued (PMI, 2013a) to state that 60% of companies surveyed evaluated improving implementation of strategic projects as high or very high. PMI Thought Leadership Series Report (2015a) continued to acknowledge that the C-suite still struggles with resource allocation and killing projects within the portfolio.

Portfolio success was predicated on four lessons learned from high-performing organizations (PMI, 2013b). The first was to have a strong, formal, disciplined approach to portfolio management. The approach had to include tying project and program implementations to strategy execution. The second was based on keeping it simple. Strategy leaders are busy, need access, and understanding of data quickly. Two simple dashboards that meet these requirements are resource requirements, by type and organization over time, and the value versus risk of projects/programs as related to strategic objectives (PMI, 2013b).

The third lesson learned was to drive a portfolio culture in the organization (PMI, 2013b). When the C-suite devoted the time and attention, supported the portfolio manager, devoted the necessary resources, and *walks the talk,* the devotion to portfolio management happens. When project leaders (PL) and project teams realize that their time is dedicated to strategic goals, then there is ownership and trust. The project teams understand when the project is finished or canceled, they will be devoted to a project that matters (PMI, 2013b).

The fourth lesson learned was to develop strong processes and procedures for portfolio management. Decision making was the key to developing strong processes (PMI, 2013b). When criteria are strong decision making maturity increases and the portfolio was the key to driving the strategy.

Müller et al.'s (2008) study recommended five portfolio practices that support the Project Management Institute Thought Leadership Series Report (2013a, 2013b). The recommended practices were as follows:

1. The portfolio's projects needed a uniformed communication practice and platform.

2. Projects should be measured with similar key performance indicators or metrics.

3. Decision making needs to occur in teams, at the organization and portfolio levels, with leaders who understand pros/cons of priorities.

4. Projects are selected based on strategy, not personal preferences.

5. Portfolios are periodically reviewed. When more than one portfolio exists need to have compatible metrics (Müller et al., 2008).

Summary

The project management discipline, when implemented, drives strategy. In other words, project and program management *does the work right*, while portfolio management *does the right work.* These phrases were coined by the PMI to help drive the project management to executives.

When projects, programs, and portfolio management are done in a coordinated fashion with strong discipline, the value is demonstrated by being able to resource projects correctly, increasing morale, helping the corporation *balance its checkbook,* and understanding when the portfolio will deliver strategic value.

With this in focus, the project management organization can assist other organizations to deliver the strategic services as well. Contracting and acquisition will have a portfolio roadmap that helps to determine the optimal time to develop strategies for contracting and acquisition. A better value may be delivered when needs of several strategic projects can be coordinated to deliver more value to the organization. Transportation and logistics will have knowledge of when product need to ship or when deliveries are needed. Reverse logistics will be part of the process as well. As projects are brought into the portfolio or even before, the reverse logistics organization can provide lessons learned, as well as define return, reuse, and even manufacturing that enhances reverse logistics.

Chapter Two—Discussion/Quiz Questions

    a. How long has project management existed?

    b. How does the PMI define the work of project management?

    c. What is PERT?

    d. What is EVM?

    e. What is C/SCSC?

    f. What is portfolio management?

    g. What is program management?

h. What differentiates portfolio/program management from project manage-ment?

i. What are the four lessons learned that define portfolio success?

j. What are three certifications offered by PMI and DAU?

CHAPTER THREE
HISTORY OF CONTRACTING AND ACQUISITION

Contracts have been around as there has been a need to exchange goods and services between different parties. Archeologists have found 5,000 year old contracts between parties where one party would supply labor and in exchange, the worker would receive certain goods, such as foodstuff and beer (Dockrill, 2016). Contracts are a way to limit the liability of parties and to protect parties from risk and the unknown. Most contracts contain clauses that also define various contingencies and details to manage known risks when they arise. For example, many years ago, it was normal to make a verbal contract with another person. Many deals were verbal "gentlemen's agreements" were made between parties that shaped the business world. Over time, agreements are far more complex and require not only to be written, but also to be examined by legal professionals to understand all the ramifications of the agreement.

Furthermore, the judicial system requires that agreements (contracts) be in writing over a certain dollar amount. Otherwise, those contracts are not enforceable. Also, an agreement that is not in writing is much riskier as both parties are then able to interpret what is expected of them. This additional risk can be mitigated by putting the contract in writing; hence, more contracts are in writing as a way to mitigate risk.

Elements of a Contract

A contract must have three essential elements: an offer, acceptance, and consideration. In addition to these three elements, a good contract should also abide by several other elements. The parties must have capacity in both age and mental capacity. The parties must have substance and not misrepresent. There must be full or accurate disclosure; there must not be a fraudulent plan; the contract cannot be for anything illegal, and neither party must have been coerced or unduly influenced to enter into the contract.

It is not a requirement that a contract is in writing, and in fact, some verbal contracts are legal and enforceable, but they are certainly riskier. One should consult the Universal Commercial Code with emphasis on the section regarding the statue of frauds as well as any other local laws when determining what contracts should be in writing. In general, if the agreement is important, one should make a contract for the relationship. Both parties will benefit from having the agreement in writing.

One way that a contract can be terminated is due to a breach of contract. Although there are several manners in which an agreement can terminate, understanding the breach of a contract is very important. Breach of contract occurs when one party does not live up to their contractual obligations. In many agreements, there will be a grievance procedure or other process where a breach can be resolved. One must be careful to understand these breach processes before taking action. If one were to take action that is not congruent with the agreement, then one can be found in breach of the agreement.

For example, Company A receives a shipment from Company B, and the inspection of the product finds that the shipment is over the agreed upon defect rate. Company A then decides not to pay Company B for the shipment but uses the products that pass inspection. The agreement states that when there is a disputed shipment then the two parties must meet and discuss a mutually agreed upon solution. If that is not done, either party can then request binding arbitration to resolve the difference. Company B then requests binding arbitration to resolve the situation, as they have not received payment for a shipment that was received and used.

In this case, the arbitrator will very likely find Company A in breach and Company B will not be found in breach. This situation may confuse many people because Company A seemed to be the company that delivered the defective goods, which caused extra rework and inspection to keep their production line moving. However, the issue is that Company A did not follow the procedure and hence was in breach. Company B might have caused a problem, but Company A did not have the right to withhold payment, even though the shipment was found to be more defective than outlined in the contract. Company A should have refused the shipment or requested a meeting to discuss a mutually agreeable solution.

Actions of Parties

Even though there are laws in place to protect individuals, one has to be careful of the parties' actions. As we discuss contracts, we understand the importance of having signed agreements in place to establish that all parties were aware of the requirements of the contract. Although this is important, it is not a requirement. It is a good idea to have signatures but if parties act as if there is an agreement in place, then it can be ruled that there be an agreement in place. Keep in mind that contract disputes will be ruled upon by the judicial system and there is room for interpretation of contracts if certain elements are left unclear. For example, a person sells their car to someone for $1,000 cash. The terms of the agreement are "as is" but both parties never sign anything. The seller signs the title of the car to the buyer and seller accepts the payment. The buyer then uses the car, and the air conditioning breaks down at 2 months, the fan belt breaks at 4 months, and finally, it totally breaks down 6 months later. The buyer comes back and asks for a refund at 6 months after not hearing from them about the other problems. The buyer would not have a good case for a refund. They used the car and for all practical purposes, it appeared that the contract stipulated "as is." Even though there was no signed agreement, both parties acted as if there was an agreement and that would become the de facto agreement.

However, after 2 months the air conditioning breaks and buyer contacts the seller and the seller pays for the repairs. In this case, it would appear that there was some guarantee given at the time of purchase. The lesson here is that one should put it in writing rather than to be at the mercy of a judge to decide the liable party.

Contract Incentives

While most people are familiar with positive incentives, such as offering a bonus for early completion, negative incentives are somewhat less common but also they can be harder to enforce. When there is a penalty clause for late or poor performance, there is too much opportunity to negotiate away that penalty. For example, a project is running late, and the vendor might want to negotiate away a negative incentive. A vendor might say to a company that if they forgo the penalty clause that they will add more people on the project and it will be done sooner and not be as late. They can position it that they will be paying overtime already, and the penalty will make the project less profitable. If the client resists, the supplier can threaten to be even later to force the additional payment for overtime.

Known and Unknown Contract Risks

Effective contracts limit the liability of parties and protect parties from risk and the unknown. Most contracts contain clauses that also define various contingencies and details to manage known risks, and offer solutions to when certain circumstances arise. An effective contract can not only address known risks but can also offer guidance or solutions for unknown risks.

In the case of known risks, most project managers are familiar with their responsibility to achieve the lowest price. Suppose that a project requires certain materials to be delivered by a certain day to a certain location. The project manager dutifully negotiates the best price possible for the product but fails to note that in the contract that the material provided is given "as is" with no warranty or guarantee after the product leaves the factory. These terms might not be a problem if the product is a low-cost, low-risk item such as a nut and bolt that is only used to hold a bracket in place for ascetic purposes and the nut and bolt are under no particular stress or engineering requirement. However, one might consider an "as is" contract as very risky for an important engineering critical element of the project. It is important that the project manager should understand the scope of work of the project to apply the correct risk mitigation to the type of agreement.

Furthermore, for known risks, the contract type can also impact risk. For example, a fixed price agreement puts more risk upon the seller as the selling party must understand all the possible risks to offer an effective bid. In general, a project manager should seek to defer as much risk as possible to others. Some projects will require the use of a time and materials contract, which essentially moves more risk to the buyer. As the seller is guaranteed a certain labor and cost markup, the risk of additional work falls upon the buyer to manage.

As for addressing unknown risks, an effective contract should include such elements as a force majeure clause. Although such a clause is common, what contract managers often fail to control is how this can be applied. In many cases, such a clause is left open and becomes subject to interpretation. Typically, in the event of a major catastrophe (war, fire, flood, earthquake, labor strike, and civil unrest) will eliminate the obligations of the contract. A major catastrophe will often leave the project manager to scramble to find an alternative supplier, however, what happens in the case of force majeure incidents that are less catastrophic. For example, a labor strike might occur at a contracted factory causing delays. A force majeure clause would relieve the seller of meeting a delivery deadline, but what if the labor strike was only for a week? The force majeure clause would relieve the seller from meeting the deadline, but given the minor nature of the delay, a prudent project manager would make sure that the contract addresses these kinds of disruptions.

To remove this kind of unknown risk, one should look at a day for day disruption clause. In the event of some unknown external event that can impact the schedule, a day of disruption can move the deadline back by a day. A day for day disruption clause allows addressing certain larger risk issues that might arise, while still preserving the contract without having an open-ended clause for the seller.

Thus, there are known and unknown contract risks and that there are methods to mitigate these kinds of situation. In some cases, the type of agreement will drive the solution while there should be clear clauses that address other unanticipated situations. In the end, an agreement needs to outline what is an acceptable and appropriate behavior to manage the actions of the parties involved to create contracts that effectively manage risk.

Summary

By law, agreements (contracts) are to be made in writing over a certain dollar amount. Otherwise, those contracts are not enforceable. Also, an agreement that is not in writing is much riskier as both parties are then able to interpret what is expected of them. Furthermore, if the agreement goes so bad that there is litigation about the situation, then there will be no record of these sidebar agreements. The risk of the oral agreement is to be vigilant about updating the contract in writing; hence, more contracts are in writing as a way to mitigate risk.

Chapter Three—Discussion/Quiz Questions

a. Have contracts been around for thousands of years?

b. What are the elements of a contract?

c. What is a verbal agreement?

d. Are there times when a contract should be written?

e. What is an offer?

f. What is acceptance?

g. What is consideration?

h. What is breach of contract?

i. What happens when a contract is terminated?

j. Why are the actions of parties important for a contract?

k. What are contract incentives?

l. What are the types of contract risks?

m. What is force majeure with relation to a contract?

CHAPTER FOUR
HISTORY OF TRANSPORTATION AND LOGISTICS

To understand global logistics, one needs to understand the logistics path from raw materials to the consumer. Although historically, there were cottage-type industries where raw materials were gathered and products created for the local marketplace, that type of system almost does not exist anymore anywhere in the world. Hence, understanding the modern history of transportation and logistics requires an understanding of intermodal transportation. Intermodal transportation involves the shipping of freight that uses multiple types of transport at the same time (Hazen & Lynch, 2008). An example would be when the material moves by rail for a portion of the shipment, and then the cargo moves to a truck for another portion of the shipment. The most common form of intermodal freight is when material moves by flat car and trailer or container (Hazen & Lynch, 2008). This chapter will examine the history of intermodal transportation and then review the various competing forms of intermodal transportation that have arisen due to significant changes in the marketplace.

History of Intermodal Transportation

The United States has gone through many changes in transportation throughout the existence of the nation. If one examines the changes in regulation and deregulation of transportation, there is a relationship between the various wars that have sought to subvert this great nation. During times of great change and strive, there is a drive by government to exert more control upon the transportation infrastructure. During times following a war, there is less of a need to exercise such governmental control. There have been several important historical events and several historical legislations passed that have impacted transportation in the United States. The following will discuss those wars, events, and significant pieces of legislation that have left their mark in the deregulation and ultimate regulation of transportation in the United States.

The first great change in modern transportation came about due to the American Civil War. This conflict created a great need for a standard and accessible transportation system in the nation. In particular, as the war raged on, the nation found that the side that had the stronger transportation infrastructure would be better able to move the men and materials necessary to be successful in battle. The American Civil War created the need for additional rail connections and in 1863, in the middle of the American Civil War, the Homestead Act was passed which was the first attempt to incentivize the construction and expansion of railroads throughout the nation (Hazen & Lynch, 2008).

This Homestead Act led rise to the large railroad companies that would dominate logistics in the United States for decades. However, it did cause issues for farmers who were forced to accept high freight costs due to the monopoly that certain railroads had upon certain lines into different cities. During this period, transportation companies, notably railroad companies grew and expanded throughout the nation. These large monopolies controlled rates and usage creating a corrupt system that favored a few and punished many. During this time there were organizations of farmers that pooled resources to combat some of the tactics employed by these colossal transportation giants.

Although the expansion of railroad track did help the trade of the nation as a whole, large railroad monopolies controlled rates creating a system of those that were favored and those that suffered. This unequal relationship between the railroads and farmers continued until the passing of Grainger Laws of the 1870s that controlled maximum rates charged and limited railroad mergers (Wisner et al., 2012).

This deregulation of the transportation industry continued for decades until the watershed Supreme Court case of *Wabash, St. Luis and Pacific Railway Company v. the State of Illinois* which moved to deregulate transportation companies and to allow the U.S. government to regulate the industry (Hazen & Lynch, 2008). Shortly after this case, in 1887 the Interstate Commerce Act was passed with the goal to regulate and control the transportation industry so that large monopolies would not dominate this important business industry. The Interstate Commerce Act prohibited certain activities, such as unjust or unreasonable charges, kickbacks, unreasonable preferences and price fixing schemes that made short haul more costly than long haul rates (Hazen & Lynch, 2008).

In the 1880s, the United States continued to take action to improve the nation's transportation infrastructure. The Interstate Commerce Act passed in 1887 was written to regulate the transportation industry. The Interstate Commerce Act sought to prohibit different corrupt practices by prohibiting them and making them illegal (Hazen & Lynch, 2008). Furthermore, by the 1900s, the United States realized that its small navy would have significant difficulties defending both oceans.

The United States, for reasons of defense, took up the cause of building the Panama Canal. This modern engineering marvel was attempted by other nations in the past. However, none was successful. When the Panama Canal was completed, this feat of engineering was considered a significant accomplishment for a nation as young as the United States. After all, France had made a significant investment in the Panama Canal project before the United States taking control of the project, and the French investment group was unsuccessful to make any significant progress. Despite the Panama Canal being built to allow the largest ships of the day to transit, the growth of ships continues to the present day. The limitation of the size of vessels that could transit the Panama Canal would in the future have a far-reaching impact on intermodal transportation.

Although transportation companies continued to grow, during pre-World War I period there was a feeling in the United States that these large companies put profits before people. During this period, there was a series of "trust busting" activities by the U.S. government along with new legislation that sought to limit these corporate giants from controlling government.

Several acts by government further regulated railroads such as the Elkins Act of 1903, Hepburn Act of 1906, and the Mann–Elkins Act of 1910 (Hazen & Lynch, 2008). All of this legislation was an attempt to control better and regulate transportation that had grown to a point where it controlled the movement of goods across the nation. Furthermore, the Interstate Commerce Commission grew in members and importance during this period.

Although this period of regulation improved costs, it reduced efficiency and by the time the United States entered World War I, the nation was unprepared to harness the transportation resources required for the material needs of this conflict. Railroads were struggling and lacked sufficient flexibility for success. In 1920, the railroads were returned to private ownership with substantially reduced government influence. Although this did improve the condition and usefulness of railroads, it was clear that motor carriers were the future of the nation.

Trucks had started to become a significant means of transporting goods around the nation, and the expansion of the use of trucks continues to the present day (Hazen & Lynch, 2008). In 1935 the first Motor Carrier Act was passed to regulate truck transportation, which had been steadily growing in the United States. The Motor Carrier Act was followed by the Civil Aeronautics Act of 1938 and the Water Carriers Act of 1940. All of these growing acts to regulate transportation became important as the United States entered into World War II.

After World War II, there was another push to regulate commerce as well as the transportation that governed this area. There is no doubt that the commerce had started to be more global during this period as people have a growing awareness of the United States as a global power on the world stage. Furthermore, during this period the United States agreed to help rebuild many of the nations that were destroyed during World War II. The increased demand for goods from the United States caused the transportation infrastructure of the nation to continue to expand past the war years, however, by 1960 the rebuilding of Europe and other nations was complete and the Korean War had come to a close.

However, the first trailer put on a flat car did not happen until 1936; it did not become a service provided by a larger carrier until 1952 (Hazen & Lynch, 2008). Once the large carriers started to market this kind of service, the service would continue to grow in importance with regard to the movement of freight throughout the nation.

In the 1960s, the U.S. government shifted from the philosophy of regulating transportation to a philosophy of deregulation. This change to deregulation ultimately led to increased transportation companies and transportation options. By 1960 there was a concerted push by the government to deregulate transportation as a whole. As there were more and more providers of freight and transportation, as cost continued to drop, and as more interstate highways allowed longer freight movement at lower costs, the government no longer found the need to regulate this industry. Presidents Kennedy and Ford both moved to reduce regulation in the transportation industry. Although it is clear that government wanted to move out of the transportation industry, it took time and several acts to dismantle the regulation that has been building up over the past several decades. It is interesting to note that during this period, in 1965, that Yale University undergraduate Frederick Smith wrote a term paper that invented the overnight shipping industry and practically revolutionized modern logistics with this concept (FEDEX, n.d.).

The shift in government's perspective of logistics led to three acts, one for railroads, one for airlines, and one for ground transportation to alter the regulations that used to control these industries. The period from 1970 to 1980 saw significant reductions in government regulation; this has allowed the transportation industry in the United States to flourish over time. This deregulation has assisted in the growth of U.S. transportation companies as well as a reduction in overall freight rates as business comes to have many different options available. This hands-off approach by the government continues to the present day where transportation companies are competing in the global marketplace. Also, there have been several new entrants into this industry as it is clear that streamlined freight rates can allow a company to be globally competitive rather than just competitive nationally, regionally, or locally. No longer in competition just the store down the street, but transportation allows the competition to be the store in China, UK, or Japan.

This shift in focus by the government led to the expansion of intermodal transportation as well as the expansion of the interstate system. This position of government deregulation continues to the present where transportation companies compete globally. The shift of government allowed the transportation industry to flourish, and more and more operations came to depend on intermodal transportation. By 2007, ~50% of intermodal traffic involved rail-transported containers and containerships (Hazen & Lynch, 2008). This number continued to rise as more and more goods are moved by ships, increasing the need for greater throughput through the Panama Canal.

Panama Canal Expansion

The expansion of the Panama Canal now allows larger containerships to transit the Panama Canal. Vessels of up to 14,000 TEUs will be able to transit through the canal (Republic of Panama, 2015). This change will certainly impact intermodal transportation. Although there is no guarantee that organizations will change their current intermodal transportation plan, there could be significant economic motivators that could change the current intermodal dynamic.

Consider that the vast majority of materials coming to the United States from the Far East enter into the Port of Los Angeles and then is moved out by rail to other cities (Inbound Logistics, 2013). There is no doubt that rail will continue to be important to landlocked cities and states. However, there is a huge market in the various East Coast Cities such as Boston, Miami, and New York. These huge cities require sizable quantities of goods to serve their large populations. Currently, this is being met through a land bridge intermodal traffic out from the Port of Los Angeles. Land bridge intermodal transportation is the combining of the ocean and rail freight that is offered as a single package by freight companies to meet the needs of their customers.

Given that larger vessels will be able to transit the Panama Canal, this will offer shipping companies opportunities to compete with current land bridge operations. Shipping companies will need to change some shipping lanes and ports of service to determine if such competition would be economically feasible. Shipping companies would need to reposition containerships to new lines of service with the hope of capturing some of the existing rail intermodal services. Although this is certainly a risk, there are significant motivations to make this shift, notably, the current low cost of fuel coupled with the lower transportation costs associated with ocean shipping.

The expansion of the Panama Canal will have an impact on intermodal transportation. With the expansion, the Panama Canal will be able to allow larger container ships to transit the canal, making sea transit from Asia to the U.S. East Coast cities possible without the involvement of railroads. This change will result in intermodal traffic that will shift from ocean transportation and long distance rail to ocean transportation and short distance truck.

Current Challenges in Transportation and Logistics

Transportation demand has become a global challenge. Although there has been much intermodal transportation in the past, the widening of the Panama Canal will further increase the transportation options available. The industry also is being challenged by upstart transportation organization with substantial funding such as Amazon. Amazon is rapidly purchasing logistics companies to bring their transportation needs in-house. The cost of transportation can be quite high and is a significant portion of an organization's spending (Boyer & Verma, 2010). Hence, there is a clear demand for a reduction in the cost of transportation as well as a drive for companies to better control the transportation infrastructure that meets their organizational needs.

Amazon Enters the Global Logistics Market

Amazon has begun an aggressive acquisition program to create a global network of logistics. Amazon seems to be breaking away from the model that they are a retail giant and moving to become a global retail solution. There is no doubt that this strategy makes sense, as Walmart has become the largest retailer in the world by leveraging a strong supply chain strategy. It is clear that Amazon is looking to use a similar strategy; however, unlike other retailers it wants to own the transportation system.

Although this may appear at the surface that intermodal transportation would simply move from one freight forwarding company to another, the difference is that Amazon has also become a manufacturer of delivery drones (Amazon, n.d.). This new technology has the potential to disrupt the old system of movement of goods. Given that large delivery, drones have just recently been approved by the Federal Aviation Administration (FAA); there are still questions regarding this technology (Associated Press, 2014). However, as with most new technologies, there needs to be greater acceptance before it can change an entire industry.

Summary

In conclusion, intermodal freight will certainly be changing over the next several years. However, when one examines the history of intermodal freight, it is not surprising that every few decades a shift occurs. The anticipated change from the expansion of the Panama Canal, as well as the disruption technology potential from Amazon, will create the next decade that will have more changes in transportation and logistics than the last one.

Chapter Four—Discussion/Quiz Questions

a. What is intermodal freight?

b. Why was the American Civil War important to logistics?

c. Explain the Homestead Act of 1863.

d. What did the Interstate Commerce Act of 1887 change in logistics?

e. Why did the United States build the Panama Canal?

f. What was the position of the U.S. government just prior to World War II?

g. Why did the U.S. government move from regulation to deregulation in the 1960s?

h. Why is intermodal freight important today?

i. What impacts with the Panama Canal expansion have upon logistics and freight?

j. What impact has Amazon had upon logistics?

k. Will drones become part of logistics in the future?

CHAPTER FIVE
HISTORY OF REVERSE LOGISTICS

The United States has gone through many changes in transportation throughout the existence of the nation. However, when one examines modern reverse logistics, most scholars would look to World War II as the turning point for retrograde military logistics. At the cease of hostilities in the aftermath of World War II, there was a growing need to draw down forces and material from Europe and the Pacific. The U.S. military pioneered the modern reverse logistics movement with the military draw down and retrograde movement of goods (military and support) back to the United States. The United States had been expanding its military presence in all theaters of war, and once hostilities ceased, there was the looming question of what should be done with all the military equipment that was now positioned far away from the United States.

After World War II, there was a push to regulate commerce as the demand for goods from the United States increased as nations raced to rebuild. There is no doubt that commerce was more global during this period as people have a growing awareness of the United States as a global power on the world stage. Furthermore, during this period, the United States agreed to help rebuild many of the destroyed nations during World War II. This global demand for U.S. products caused the transportation infrastructure of the nation to continue to expand past the war years; however, by 1960, the rebuilding of Europe and other nations was complete and the Korean War had come to a close.

Deregulation

By 1960, there was a concerted push by the government to deregulate transportation as a whole. As there were more and more providers of freight and transportation, as cost continued to drop, and as more interstate highways allowed longer freight movement at lower costs, the government no longer found the need to regulate this industry. This decrease in costs of transportation led to the possibility of returned goods as a cost-effective means of addressing a problem. This deregulation has assisted in the growth of U.S. transportation companies as well as a reduction in overall freight rates as business comes to have many different options available. The position of the United States government deregulating the transportation industry continues to the present day where transportation companies are competing in the global marketplace. Lowered costs of freight allow for economic returns and create an economically viable platform for reverse logistics.

The Value of Reverse Logistics

The reported value of U.S. returns is estimated at 100 billion per year and consists of ~4% of the U.S. GDP (Blanchard, 2012; Li & Olorunniwo, 2008; Stock & Mulki, 2009). This statistic alone shows the importance of the management of returns. Further studies have shown that the rate of returns can vary between 5% and 50% (Rogers & Tibben-Lembke, 1998) and so even at a modest 5% rate, this level of returns is significant.

If one were to assume that 5% of a company's value is tied up in a process that can have serious brand ramifications, this alone should be sufficient for an organization to address this significant issue. Given the reduction of margins in the current competitive marketplace, 5% can be the difference between long-term success and short-term failure. If a highly efficient organization can achieve a 0.5% returns, (1 in 200), this is significantly >0.00034% (3.4 per million) that Six Sigma promised to deliver. Clearly, there is more at work than just quality with regard to returns, and hence organizations should take notice of this situation and apply management solutions to achieve a clear competitive advantage.

The reason that most organizations are unwilling to invest into a better returns or repairs process is many organizations feel that returns or repairs cut into the revenue stream. Organizations might ignore the rate or returns because there is the idea that there are often mitigating circumstance regarding returns. High rates of returns can be an indication of greater problems beyond quality. Additionally, even low rates of return can be a problem because poorly handled returns can result in long-term customer service issues, which are often not reported because some organizations equate all quality issues with returns. A natural response might be to blame all returns upon quality issues without looking into the situation further. Furthermore, organizations feel that returns expend organizational energy without any return, which is in effect best, a return is a negative revenue. Another common issue is that most companies will know their revenue numbers and manufacturing throughput, but few will track returns.

The few organizations that do track these returns often only track returns as a negative to sales and so little analysis will go into understanding why the returns occurred in the first place. What is often overlooked is that returns happen more frequently than organizations want to admit. Despite improving quality, returns continue to happen, and part of the reason is the lack of understanding how to use the product by the consumer (Blanchard, 2012).

Reverse logistics studies have shown that there is a portion of returned products that are tested, but the company fails to identify any issue with the product (Stock, 2001). These "no fault returns" cost a company money, time, and prestige. Interestingly, these "no fault returns" will often outnumber the quantity returned for actual quality issues, yet few organizations try to learn what the cause of these types of returns is (Stock, 2001).

Despite these problems, because non-quality issues are often not tracked, most organizations remain ignorant to the real problem with their returns. Given the volume of these "no fault returns," one needs to consider the implications for the returns process. One notable exception to this rule is Hitachi America. Blanchard (2012) reports that Hitachi America reduced service calls to consumers by 33% by implementing a service call avoidance program to help consumers fix the problem. This service call avoidance program used a technical services hotline to assist consumers in walking through and addressing some problems. This program reduced costs by eliminating needless service calls to consumers.

The Present

There have been many new entrants into the transportation industry as it is clear that streamlined freight rates can allow a company to be globally competitive rather than just competitive nationally, regionally, or locally. The Internet has created a demand for transportation services from the growing number of e-retailers (Fernie & Sparks, 2014). There are an estimated 5 billion users of the Internet, and many of that traffic are for the purchase of goods, which in turn require transportation for delivery to the client (Fernie &

Sparks, 2014). With so much global demand for transportation is it any wonder that retail giants like Amazon are looking to develop their global logistics network. Companies today understand that the cost of goods in transportation costs organizations money (Boyer & Verma, 2010). Hence, there is a clear demand for a reduction of the time in transit of all goods so transportation companies will continue to seek to bring new value to its customers.

Summary

Ultimately, the pendulum of regulation and deregulation has swung again in the United States as deregulation is allowing transportation companies to compete worldwide. Deregulation appears to allow for greater efficiencies in the transportation industry. This clear change in the direction of legislation in the United States will allow transportation to be a growth sector for many years to come. As long as transportation companies avoid abuses and corrupt practices, there is no doubt that the government will remain out of the transportation industry.

Chapter Five—Discussion/Quiz Questions

a. Explain reverse logistics.

b. What impact did World War II have upon reverse logistics?

c. How did deregulation of transportation impact reverse logistics?

d. What is the value of reverse logistics?

e. Why is managing returns so important to a company?

f. Is quality the major reason for returns?

g. Why should organizations track their returns?

h. Can companies save money by improving their returns process?

i. Will technology change reverse logistics in the future?

CHAPTER SIX
SUMMARY

When one looks back on the history of contracts, transportation, logistics, and reverse logistics, there was a great turning point with regard to freight with the invention of containerized freight. Containerized freight offered a new revolution for cargo that changed the way products moved around the world. In the past, all ship cargo moved from place to place in a bulk format. Although this did maximize the use of irregular-sized ships compartments, the move to containers allowed the movement of product from place to place in an organized and controlled manner. It did require the adoption of specialized technologies. However, the shift changed how trains and trucks also moved products. Containerization proved to be so successful that this revolution required rail and trucks to adapt to move containers. With containers, cargo could move directly from the ship to an awaiting truck or rail can and then allow the material to move onward to their destination without additional handling. The elimination of additional handling allows the material to move from ships to retailers by containers. Despite containers still being the dominant method to move cargo, the new driver of containerized cargo will be autonomous technology.

To this end, autonomous technology is already present in some areas and will continue to change and evolve how cargo will move from the point of manufacturing to the point of consumption. New logistics technology is already changing how cargo moves in ports due to the move to utilize robots in the loading and unloading of containerized cargo in key high-throughput terminals. Industrial robots have been common in many other industries, and they have been proven effective in manufacturing as well as in distribution. Autonomous robots will perform repetitive tasks, such as loading and unloading ships. Autonomous robots will change the operation of terminals as they will be able to operate around the clock without concerns about human fatigue that can set in. Also, these autonomous robots will require less human control and so there will be efficiencies that result in streamlining of costs.

Sure, this sounds like science fiction, but the technology of this type is already science fact. One might wonder when will one expect to see robots unloading ships, and in fact, it is already taking place. One of the busiest ports in the United States, the Port of Los Angeles, is already piloting the use of robots (Lippert, 2016). Self-driving cranes have already been unloading containerized cargo with hardly anyone noticing. Self-driving cranes operate at 18 mph and can operate around the clock with minimal human intervention (Lippert, 2016). This kind of disruptive technology will not only change the way freight it handled, but will also revolutionize logistics.

If the application of autonomous technology in terminal operations is not enough, there are already companies working to create self-piloting ships. The media has already been hyping the arrival of self-piloting automation, such as demonstrated by the Google car. Self-piloting technology has been highlighted in the news a lot, due to efforts by Google and Amazon. However, most people have not considered the application of this technology to ships. Unlike cars, ships operate in vast oceans with a lot fewer obstacles than a car trying to navigate the streets of a city like London or Hong Kong. Although people have not been paying as much attention to this area, there are already autonomous vessels in current operation. Container operators like Hapag–Lloyd are already developing technology to create autonomous vessels shortly (Hapag-Lloyd, n.d.). The U.S. Navy has already launched the Sea Hunter, which is an autonomous vessel that detects and monitors submarine activity (Larter, 2016). Although there are several companies working on the technology, it is clear that legislation will need to change to allow commercial vessels to operate unmanned. Of course, now that the U.S. Navy is already moving forward with this technology, it is only a matter of time before the commercial side moves ahead with this technology.

Critics would be quick to point out that operating a single vessel in the open ocean is different from operating a vessel in a busy channel like at the entry point for many ports. Keeping dozens of ships from a collision is a much different technology than cruise control on a car. To this end, the U.S. Navy has contracted with a provider that has been working with swarm boats for some time (MAREX, 2014). The United States has already been working with the operation of numerous autonomous vessels in the same general area. These swarm boats not only operate independently, but they can also operate with the goal to surround another ship for a tactical advantage (MAREX, 2014). The application of this technology shows that dozens of autonomous vessels can operate together in a small area and avoid a collision.

When one compares autonomous robots and autonomous ships, these technologies are part of the same family of technologies that will change logistics for many years to come. The technology that keeps autonomous ships from colliding will be similar to the technology that keeps autonomous container cranes from colliding. One would expect that the autonomous ship technology will be more complicated than autonomous crane technology as cranes operate on specific tracks. However, they do become part of the same whole because once these technologies reach a tipping point, they will become common throughout the world. Once the tipping point happens, there will be increases in cargo efficiency that has never been thought to be possible. There will be many people who do not want to relinquish this kind of control to computers. However, the fact remains that the majority of shipping incidents are due to errors in human judgment. Even the most intelligent person on the planet is subject to momentary lapses in judgment that can cause an accident, which does not happen to a machine. Taking it a step further, when two autonomous vehicles are on a collision course, it is possible for those entities to communicate and collaborate in a manner to avoid a collision. Collaboration and communication between drivers of vehicles are not possible at the speed in which computers can manage.

As of today, the autonomous robots in the Port of Los Angeles, the USN Sea Hunter, and swarm boats are all pilot projects; however, they are heralding new changes in ports and shipping. These autonomous programs will become perfected over time and will lead to greater innovation. Although there will be setbacks, cost constraints, and possible legislation that will modify the speed of growth and adoption of this technology, there is no way to put the genie back in the bottle. Furthermore, if the United States does not move ahead with these technologies, there is no doubt that other nations will move ahead with these technologies. Time will certainly tell what nation will be the first to perfect the technology. However, these early applications prove that port operations are ripe for change.

In closing, the application of self-piloting technologies is going to revolutionize ports and ships. Some might feel uncomfortable with this technology; however, it will be a matter of time and cost that will eventually win over the critics of these technologies. The shift has already been happening for some time and although there will be those that resist the technology, sooner or later, the cost advantage of the application of this type of technology is going to overcome the resistance of those who want to keep things as they have been in the past.

Chapter Six—Discussion/Quiz Questions

a. Has history reached a great turning point?

b. Will technology change our lives at many different levels in the future?

c. Is society ready for all this change?

d. Will contracts change in the future due to new technology? Why or why not?

e. Will logistics and transportation change in the future due to new technology? Why or why not?

f. Will reverse logistics change in the future due to new technology? Why or why not?

g. Does the United States have the ability to remain ahead of other nations with this changing technology?

h. How will these new technologies impact society, ethics, and culture?

i. Will this change be larger than the change that happened with the invention of the SMART phone?

SECTION TWO
PROJECT MANAGEMENT PERSPECTIVES

CHAPTER SEVEN
INTER-RELATIONSHIP OF PROJECT MANAGEMENT AND CONTRACTING AND ACQUISITION

Contracting and acquisition in the U.S. government are heavily regulated. The overarching regulation is called the Federal Acquisition Regulation (FAR) and within the Department of Defense, there is the DFARS (Department of Defense Federal Acquisition Regulation Supplement). Many of the other federal agencies also have a version of the FARs. The agencies FARs are addenda to the basic FARs. The agencies regulations cannot be any less stringent than the basic FARS.

FARs were generated as a result of Federal agencies not having consistent rules and processes. Once the FARs became law, as improprieties occurred the FARs would be updated. The updates continue to this day. While some of the changes are due to improprieties, many of the updates are helping streamline the process of contracting and acquisition.

A government proposal let for bid has several sections. Each section is always the same. For example, section C is the statement of work. For a proposal manager and the project manager section C is quite important as it outlines the work. Where many project managers fall into a trap is that they do not review the entire proposal.

Why would this be a trap? The project manager needs to understand anything that affects the proposal and the resulting contract. For example, the terms of payment are not in section C. Let us consider, the payment terms are not within the capabilities of one's company's billing system. If it is within the proposal, it will most likely be in the final contract.

The FARs also oversees contracting. The structure of the contract is similar to that of the proposal. When the project manager is assigned to the contract, he or she is responsible for reading the contract from the first page to the last page. Any items that may affect the project need to be accounted for the work breakdown structure (WBS) and for the schedule.

For example, when an invoice needs to be generated manually, that takes effort. This effort needs to be accounted for within the WBS and the schedule. In the WBS, so it is not forgotten about; and in the schedule, so the proper resources are allocated. A requirements matrix should be developed. The requirements matrix helps the project manager dissect the contract.

The requirements matrix maps all obligations from the contract to the WBS and the schedule. The matrix map provides a forward and backward pass to make sure the completion of all the contract elements. The WBS needs to be quality checked by someone other than the project manager. This system of double verification helps to ensure that nothing gets overlooked.

Once the contract is signed, the project manager is responsible for ensuring the project team and the client stay within the scope of the contract. The project manager should prepare change requests when the clients want something outside of the scope of the contract. Negotiations may have to take place or the client may reject the change control.

When a project manager receives an approved change order, there are several steps in the process that need to be taken. The project manager reviews the change order, determines what documents if any need require changes, and updates the requirement matrix. The project manager needs to review the schedule and see if it is affected by the change order. If it is, then a new baseline is established once the change is implemented into the schedule. Financials need to be updated as well. The project manager needs to have created a monthly budget based on the contract and when expenses are expected to be received.

With regard to the financials, there are two important inter-related concepts that impact project managers. Project management and contracts and acquisition are two inter-related concepts that intersect at two important points. The first point of financial interest is returned. Although every contract is written expecting 100% fill rate and 100% perfect deliveries, there are going to be materials that are not up to specification or were damaged somewhere along the supply chain and required return (and likely replacement). The second point of intersection is warehousing. The warehouse is the project manager's nightmare because the material that sits is money that cannot be used and the more that remains in the warehouse, the greater the carrying costs of the material. An important concept of inventory in a warehouse is shrinkage because the material can only be lost and once it is lost it needs to be replaced.

Returns

Returns are a fact of any business, and an organization should seek to mitigate these wherever possible. No matter how detailed the contract, there will be material that needs to be packed up and shipped back to the vendor due to some issue. This problem then becomes a logistics and reverse logistics issue. Many organizations are under the impression that if they contract for the highest quality products they will not have any returns. Many project managers falsely believe that controlling the quality of the product is the only means to control some returns. In practice, this is not the case as there are typically more returns due to other factors than quality.

In many cases, the reason for the return is unclear as many organizations simply ignore the returns as long as the returns are not quality related or highly visible to the media (Stock, 2001). For a project to remain competitive, the project manager should move away from the mindset of just focusing on quality. The project manager should seek to understand the entire contact–logistics–reverse logistics process. Too many organizations fail to accept that the process to move product from the point of origin to the point of consumption (traditional supply chain) is different from the process to move the product from the point of consumption to the point of origin (reverse logistics).

Traditional supply chains have skilled negotiators and professional managers to control the contract and hence the flow of materials to an organization (Garrett, 2010). The use of skilled and highly specialized individuals is essential in maintaining a smooth flow of goods (and services) to a project (Slack, Chambers, & Johnson, 2010). The use of professional contract managers will also support operations in a manner to manage inbound quality. Organizations have long understood that having a highly trained and professional supply chain group will yield organizational benefits beyond the cost of these professionals. What many organizations are only beginning to realize that applying the same level of training and professionalism to returns can yield the same level (if not greater) of benefits.

In closing, the current research in returns management has shown that the responsibility should be given to a senior level management professional with specialized skills (Stock & Mulki, 2009). Furthermore, once a senior level management professional is responsible, the returns and repairs can be managed in a cost-effective manner. Because there is a budgetary implication, it only follows that there should be a department head that will do their best to limit or mitigate these costs, just as there is an executive in charge of the supply chain function or just as there is an executive in charge of operations. It might be possible to try to incorporate these responsibilities with another department but what makes warranty and service return logistics is different from the cost containment used in forward logistics or customer order fulfillment.

Warehousing

Warehouses are peculiar operations designed to hold materials until needed by the project. In many organizations, warehouse operations are referred to distribution centers to indicate that these organizations are for short-term storage rather than long-term storage (Blanchard, 2010). The reason for this is that materials in a warehouse should be moving out on a regular basis because the material that just sits in a location for an extended period costs money and is also subject to expiration. Despite these issues, warehouses offer many benefits to organizations as it allows the storage of material until needed rather than the organization waiting for material.

Cost is a factor with regard to any warehouse operation as money that is sitting on a shelf is money that is not working for the company. If a product is not being used or sold, then there is no value to anyone for the product to remain on the shelves. Consider the can of anchovies on the shelf of the supermarket. A few people might purchase this item, but it certainly would not be sold as often as something like apples. To this end, a supermarket might keep very few cans of anchovies in a warehouse while a supermarket might be moving pallets of apples in a single day. Understanding inventory levels is important for any organization because if one understands the frequency of use of products, one can better forecast needs rather than to just put inventory in stock in hopes that one day it would sell.

Warehouses benefit customers by ensuring that material is available when needed. In many operations, a product is needed quickly and having material in stock at a warehouse can help secure that sale because the item is available. When a person goes shopping for something in a store, people have a tendency to purchase what is available right away, rather than to special order goods and wait. Customers looking for one item that finds it is not available will very likely purchase a like product rather than to wait to order the initial item. Society has become very much an instant gratification society, and so having the right balance of materials in a warehouse can mean the difference between a sale today and having a customer shop elsewhere.

In closing, warehouse operations certainly have an impact on customers and organizations that can balance supply and demand of goods that can save money by keeping a minimal inventory but maximize sales by capturing the immediate demand for goods today. An organization needs to find the correct balance between products in stock and the movement of those products from the warehouse. In business, any material that remains in the warehouse unsold costs a company not only for the cost of the good but for the cost of the return that money could have generated elsewhere.

Chapter Seven—Discussion/Quiz Questions

a. What section in the proposal and contract describe the work that is required on a contract?

b. In a proposal and contract, what does the statement of work provide?

c. What parts of the proposal does a project manager need to know?

d. What is a requirements matrix?

e. When should a project manager start a change request?

f. When a change request is approved, what should a project manager do?

g. What is the purpose of a requirements matrix?

h. What is the purpose of a schedule?

i. What is a common trap that a project manager may fall into?

j. What are the FARs?

k. Why are returns important?

l. Do specialized people with specialized skills make more of an organizational impact? Why or why not?

m. Why are warehouses important to a project?

n. Should the cost of warehousing be a consideration for a project?

CHAPTER EIGHT
INTER-RELATIONSHIP OF PROJECT MANAGEMENT AND TRANSPORTATION AND LOGISTICS

Transportation and logistics in any project require an understanding of certain terms in logistics as well as the risks associated with transportation. Although the contract might clearly spell out the responsibilities of the parties, first one should understand what the technical, logistical terms mean, and second, one is expected to understand the risks associated with transportation in the project. Transportation and logistics is an interesting aspect because there are specific times when title passes from the seller to the buyer and understanding those terms are essential to the successful management of transportation and logistics in a project.

First, one should understand the legal terminology of Incoterms. There are several different Incoterms used in United States and international logistics, so having an understanding of the most common terms is the best place to start. Although there are dozens of terms, only a handful is typically used and in many cases, some of the terms are only used in very specialized cases of transportation.

The most common Incoterm is FOB (commonly known as free on board) origin. FOB origin is when title passes to the buyer at the point of origin of the product. This term means that the buyer is responsible for all freight, insurance, duties, and other fees from that origin point. More likely, one will be purchasing those spare parts FOB origin, where the origin point will be a mutually agreed warehouse location in the United States, such as FOB Los Angeles. The seller has then taken care of the freight and other costs incurred to move the project from Japan to Los Angeles and that price is likely part of the purchase price of the goods. A shipper should use FOB origin when they would like to take control of the goods at an agreed upon location where they have freight service—a consolidation point for example. This Incoterm would allow the shipper to control the cost of freight, insurance, and other fees rather than rely upon the seller who may likely mark up these costs.

Ex Works is an important Incoterm that is often confused with FOB origin. The Incoterm Ex Works is where title passes at the point of manufacture of the product. Note that this sounds similar to FOB origin; however, the location of manufacture may not be the same location as where a company might be offering the product. This similarity leads to confusion, and could lead to costly mistakes. For example, if one purchases a spare part from Honda Ex Works, then the buyer agrees to be responsible for the product at the manufacturing facility in Japan. When one purchases a part from a local Honda dealership, then one is purchasing the product FOB origin where the origin point is the local Honda dealership.

Another common Incoterm is FOB destination. FOB destination is when the seller will pay for all costs to deliver the product to a particular destination that is mutually agreed. For example, Honda parts might be purchased FOB Houston, and the seller is responsible for all costs to have the product available in Huston. The title then passes to the buyer at the point of destination, and so the seller is responsible for all freight, duties, insurance, and other costs until the product arrives at the agreed upon location. The buyer should consider this option then they want the convenience of having the product at a destination at a particular time. FOB destination would often be how to arrange a just-in-time (JIT) agreement as to keep the seller out of problems that might occur in transit because the seller would want greater control of that situation.

When one is reviewing risks in a project, it is important to address the different risks associated with transportation and logistics. This area is often out of the control of the project manager and might involve a freight forwarder, customs broker, or perhaps a third-party logistics provider. Regardless of what organization is handling the logistics, when analyzing risk, organizations may look at qualitative and quantitative risk reviews. Both types of risk reviews can assist with identifying and treating risk. Qualitative risk means to brainstorm ideas, possibly perform a strengths, weaknesses, opportunities, and threats (SWOT) analysis, or consult subject matter experts (Schwalbe, 2011). Quantitative review means to review actual data on risks and the treatment or risks (Creswell, 2003). This review could be data from past projects or related projects where the project manager has historical data to parse. Although project managers can do both, the challenge is having the resources and the time. If resources and time were available, a project manager should do both to get the best possible treatment of risk. However, in most cases, resources and time are at a premium and so the project manager will often have to make a judgment call on which to use.

Qualitative risk analysis is done when the data about the risks is not fully available. Because there are no specific data available, then it means that one needs to consider the opinions of others. The opinions of others will need to be used because there is no other information. When there are some data available, it is a good idea to consult the experts. Consulting other experts can open up new possibilities to risk review.

If there are historical examples of similar projects, then the project manager would likely be able to perform a quantitative risk review based upon existing information. This review means the examination of statistical data and other information, and one can generate a model for the likely risks. Typically, a data analysis is considered more reliable than one that is more subjective; however, that quality of the data will determine the success or failure of the risk analysis.

Using data or using opinions or doing both will not mean the identification of all risks will. However, it does help ensure that more risks are covered than by not using either type of risk review. The challenge becomes to be able to address as many risks as possible. In the end, it is better to spend a little more time in risk identification and treatment than to have to deal with so many risks in an ad hoc method during a project.

Summary

In closing, understanding the terms and risks associated with logistics is significantly important for a project. Many times a project might be able to control costs, but due to inaccurate planning the logistics and transportation costs are not properly factored into the project. This error can lead to significant overruns as freight costs are not cheap, particularly overnight or expedited freight costs that are not originally considered.

Chapter Eight—Discussion/Quiz Questions

   a. Explain Incoterms.

   b. Define FOB origin.

c. Define FOB destination.

d. Define Ex Works.

e. Explain qualitative risk.

f. Explain quantitative risk.

g. Why is risk identification important?

h. Why is risk assessment important?

i. How can one use historically similar projects with regard to risk assessment?

CHAPTER NINE

INTER-RELATIONSHIP OF PROJECT MANAGEMENT AND REVERSE LOGISTICS

Reverse logistics management (RLM) is about the handling of materials after they have been purchased for the project. Most projects will require that when considerable amounts of material will be purchased it is important to pay attention to the impact of RLM. To achieve this someone in the project should conduct an analysis of the waste stream to determine what could be returned, what could be reclaimed, and what could be recycled.

Returns, reclaimed goods, and recycling (RL3) and all important to examine determine what areas of opportunity exist. A large project could have hundreds of millions of dollars of material purchases. Taking a conservative estimate and considering that 1% of a hundred million dollar project consists of waste and recyclables, a hundred million dollar project has a 1 million dollar opportunity when it comes to recycling and reuse of materials.

Returns

The reported value of U.S. returns is estimated at 100 billion per year and consists of ~4% of the U.S. GDP (Blanchard, 2012; Li & Olorunniwo, 2008; Stock & Mulki, 2009). This statistic alone shows the importance of the management of returns. Further studies have shown that the rate of returns can vary between 5% and 50% (Rogers & Tibben-Lembke, 1998) and so even at a modest 5% rate, this level of returns is significant. Given this level of potential, any project should start with a manageable process to address returns. What often happens is that returns have many more processes or steps and so are less effective than traditional forward logistics which leads to more money lost through inefficiency.

The returns process is the most commonly identified aspect of reverse logistics. Many organizations have not defined this process, and so there is considerable room for improvement (Blanchard, 2012). An improperly established returns process can cost the company money while a streamlined returns process can save the company money. The use of a tracking number can help improve the returns process in much the same way as an invoice number tracks goods moving to the customer. If a credit is given with no product returned, then that means the organization will lose the full cost of the item.

Recycling

Recycling is the reuse of the raw material of the item. Examples of recycling are cardboard recycling, aluminum recycling, and plastic recycling. Raw materials are recycled and reused in some manner. Some states offer a refund or return value for returning the items for recycling (such as in Oregon or California). This deposit comes from the consumer at the time of the sale. The deposit goes to whoever returns the product to the recycling center. There is also a growth of cell phone recycling as there are certain important trace materials in phones that could be used to build new cell phones in the future.

Reclaimed Goods

Reclaimed goods are materials that are either re-sold in a used state to gain back some value, such as selling old computers, or sold for scrap, such as the sale of old cell phones. In many cases, because old cell phones might just mean a recent model that someone has upgraded from, there are still usable pieces that could be used in other technologies. Both of these types of reclaimed goods are important in a project. However, they should be treated differently. Also, the volume will play an important role in what makes sense to reclaim and what does not. The larger the volume of goods, the more opportunity there is for reclaiming.

As public awareness of the environment is at an all-time high, more project managers need to take visible steps toward preserving the environment. There are certainly more political and social pressures to preserve the environment, and all government agencies are required to show some level of recycling and environmental consciousness. Every project will be different, but there should be a plan to address these opportunities. Without a plan, the organization is at risk of being exposed as being an active polluter that has not taken the environment into account.

There are three best practices that stand out with regard to recycling or reclaiming material. Three best practices are to appoint a passionate person, make all changes sustainable, and to reduce the carbon footprint of the project or organization. Each of these is important and will be addressed individually.

The first best practice is to appoint a passionate person that is interested in environmental preservation. Appointing a person that will be accountable can move the organization toward greater environmental preservation. The person does not need to be a top manager because if the person is passionate, he will find time to speak to stakeholders that can make the difference. An organization should not be satisfied with just putting colored bins out in the hopes that people will recycle. It will take training and education to get people involved and interested in the program.

The second best practice is making all changes sustainable. Do not set a high expectation without proper resources. Make sure that the project has the time, the people, and the enthusiasm to manage the program. Just like in a project, one needs to consider the scope of the recycling or reclaimed goods. High volumes might require a liquidation company to assist with finding buyers for recycled or reclaimed goods (Rogers & Tibbens-Lembke, 1998).

The third best practice should be to consider the carbon footprint of the project. There might be opportunities for energy efficient buildings, energy efficient technology and the use of alternative energy sources to attain a carbon zero footprint (Gordon, 2011). One company recently announced that it would purchase a new Tesla for all new employees because the new hires would be expected to be driving and traveling as part of their job. Many municipalities have moved their buses to operate on alternative fuels to bring down emissions. There is no reason that this cannot be achieved in a long-term project as well.

Summary

RLM is essential because it can better utilize project resources. Because a project can span years, a longer time should be examined. The longer the duration of the project, the more used resources will be available at the end. Long-term considerations regarding returns, recycling, and reclaimed goods should be part of any project plan. Also, leveraging alternative renewable energy sources can also achieve reductions in energy and water requirements (Gordon, 2011). The optimization of resources and new technology make it possible to achieve remarkable savings compared to not considering those possibilities.

Chapter Nine—Discussion/Quiz Questions

a. Why is reverse logistics important to project management?

b. Explain why returns are a part of projects?

c. Why are reclaimed goods important for a project?

d. Why is recycling an important aspect of a project?

e. What is the value of a control or tracking number in the returns process?

f. What is the ethical quandary involved with recycling?

g. Should a project manager consider how goods could be reused after the conclusion of a project? Why or why not?

h. What are the three best practices with regard to recycling or reclaiming goods?

i. Why is training and education important for a recycling or reclaiming program?

j. Should a project manager be concerned about sustainability?

CHAPTER TEN
SUMMARY

Maintaining trust and good communication are becoming two of the forgotten elements of a successful supply chain. Supply chain managers are getting so busy that they are beginning to ignore the importance of the fundamentals. When supply chain managers forget the basic building blocks of organizational success, they have a difficult time finding success. Social skills are just as important as factors such as cost, scope, and schedule. If the right people are not being managed correctly, there will be strife, confusion, or worse, conscious or unconscious sabotage. Maintaining trust and communication is the only clear path to success (Figure 1).

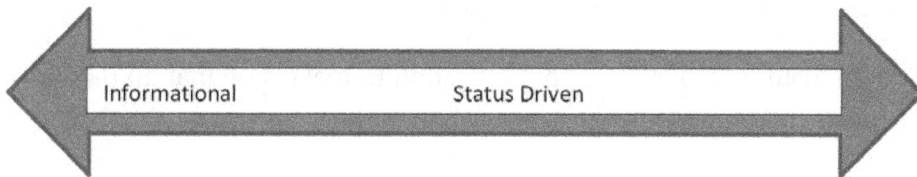

Informational   Status Driven

Figure 1: Communication types

Because supply chain managers are pressed for time and results, they gravitate toward using the same individuals and resources for similar tasks, however, over time even these kinds of relationships start to fall apart. A finely tuned machine will ultimately fail without regular maintenance. This situation is even more apparent in people where relationships are ignored or worse taken for granted for too long. Supply chain managers often fail to grasp the importance of trust on a project and instead focus on the results (or lack of results) without looking further to find out why the people were not successful. Budgets, deadlines, obstacles, stakeholders, and other situations overtake the organization, and the supply chain manager becomes without the time necessary to devote to the soft skill necessary for a successful project. Trust is built over time through positive communication.

There is no sure way to create trust, but if a supply chain manager is attentive to the communication and social needs of the project team, it will go a long way to foster success.

In closing, if a supply chain manager has time for making calls to find out status, the supply chain manager has time to maintain a positive and trusting relationship with everyone on the team. The supply chain manager should keep in mind that earning trust is important, and they must consider what they are doing to earn the trust of others on a continual basis. To this end, when trust is part of the daily agenda of the organization, then it becomes an organizational priority.

Chapter Ten—Discussion/Quiz Questions

a. Why is trust important?

b. Does a supply chain manager need to work on communication?

c. Does communication matter in a supply chain?

d. Should there be a plan for communication to make sure that all parties have the necessary information for successful cooperation?

SECTION THREE
PROGRAM MANAGEMENT PERSPECTIVES

CHAPTER ELEVEN
INTER-RELATIONSHIP OF PROGRAM MANAGEMENT AND CONTRACTING AND ACQUISITION

Program success is often based on the fulfillment of customer requirements in a certain period while remaining under a certain budget. The theory of constraints explains that scope, schedule, and budget are three of the most important aspects of any project and if one of these elements changes then it will likely have an impact on another aspect (PMBOK, 2008, pp. 6–7). What the theory of constraints does not explain is how much is the program impacted. Many people believe that the impact is proportional to the change; however, this is not the case. A resourceful program manager should understand human behavior and motivation more than schedule and budget to manage a program.

The first aspect of schedule that a program manager should realize is that there is no single set of processes or procedures to handle any given situation. Accepting that there was no one set of processes to address a program allows the program manager to break away from a linear thinking paradigm. There are times where a linear solution is not the best solution to any given problem. This shift from a single solution thinking has been an awakening for many program managers who have been trained as project managers who believe that there is one right solution. Many times the solution that should be considered revolves around the people on the project. The project manager needs to consider if the right people are in the right place and given enough authority to be successful?

Humans exist in an open system whereas traditional human thought breaks down a system into smaller parts. Western thought rests upon an understanding that everything in the universe is a discreet system rather than a complex interconnected system. Experienced program managers realize that every aspect of every project that is part of the portfolio cannot be controlled. Program managers should regularly give more authority to individuals to allow the project managers to address their project's issues. A single program leader can motivate each in a project through direct and indirect actions. An interesting thing about people is that most of the time, positive contributions, such as compliments or recognition of a job well done, can build to create something greater for the project. A leader who can offer small praises that matter can yield better results than one who is quick to criticize.

An impatient client could become hostile due to a lack of results. An experienced project manager understands that an impatient client can create a need for the completion of certain activities that is out of sequence with the project timeline. A linear project manager might find themselves paralyzed and be forced to offer excuses. However, there are times where this kind of forced requirement could push a project manager to handle issues out of sequence to achieve higher level milestones (Curlee & Gordon, 2010). Pressure like this can sometimes achieve quicker results. It could lead to the implementation of a new process that will accelerate the project timeline. Innovation can make a project successful even when those innovations do not appear on a Gantt chart.

In closing, program managers have opportunities in many different areas. There are opportunities in the process but also in the more important area, in people. Programs and projects span long periods of time so understanding people can make the difference between success and failure.

Chapter Eleven—Discussion/Quiz Questions

   a. What are some of the factors in program success?

   b. Explain the theory of constraints.

   c. Why is the theory of constraints so important to a project and to a program?

   d. How much authority should a program manager give to a project manager?

   e. Is a project or program considered an open or closed system?

   f. Explain linear thinking.

   g. Is linear thinking good or bad for a project? Why?

CHAPTER TWELVE
INTER-RELATIONSHIP OF PROGRAM MANAGEMENT AND TRANSPORTATION AND LOGISTICS

One of the large intersections of program management and transportation and logistics is metrics. A metrics is a manner to monitor any aspect of a program or project. An experienced program manager needs to understand the important logistics metrics to follow the program. To illustrate these intersections, this section will follow the progress of a typical shipbuilding program.

According to Turban, King, Lee, Liang, and Turban (2012), a "metric is a specific, measurable standard against which actual performance is compared" (p. 632). In shipbuilding, there are many metrics used to determine the actual progress of the project versus timeline. In one shipbuilding project, to keep track of progress, the project manager required the tracking of several metrics to evaluate progress. One important metric was tracking the number of major block steel assemblies. There were 50 major blocks needed to complete the vessel, and so monitoring the completion of these blocks against the original timeline provided by the shipyard was essential. By tracking actual progress against the original timeline, as well as monitoring the progression of each block, was used to estimate the actual completion date. In the end, the project did monitor several different metric; however, there are three different ones will be examined in depth to explain the importance and value of metrics management.

Although there are many aspects of shipbuilding, this chapter will only review the steel work required to build the superstructure of the vessel. In this shipbuilding project, the steel work was estimated to be 40 million dollars for a 200 million dollar ship. From the original timeline provided by the shipyard, the steel work should take 12 months to complete. These details become the baseline comparison for the project, as explained in greater detail shortly.

As previously stated, in this particular project, there were 50 major blocks that would make up the ship. In rough numbers, this means that the shipyard needed to put up a block a week to remain on schedule. For tracking purposes, blocks were considered 100% complete when they were lifted and attached. Smaller completion percentages were used for partial work in 25% increments. Given that the fast rule is one block needed completion per week, the project manager can look out the window and count the blocks and know where he stood.

The challenge for the program manager was that one would need to track the progress for each of the 50 blocks. Tracking at the block level, one can then roll up progress to see where the project was falling behind. Just counting blocks tells the project manager that the project was behind, but the question that was critical to the program manager was would it be possible for the shipyard to catch up. These last two points became critical for the project's success.

The project team monitored blocks from the time the raw materials arrived at the shipyard to the time the block was put up. Each important step in the progress was tracked to understand potential delays. Monitoring each block would allow tracking the trend and the direction that the shipyard was taking. One could also observe and track where the work would pile up to see some of the delays. Tracking at this level means knowing exactly where all the pieces are so when the program manager enters into a status meeting, the project manager has empirical proof. When the shipyard would emphatically say that they will catch up, the project manager could counter and say, there is no way to catch up because there are not enough blocks in progress to catch up.

Ahead are three metrics that have been recreated to show how they were used in the project. The tracking and details have been simplified, but they do offer a good idea regaring progress. The actual models were quite large, and there was a full-time financial analyst, who gathered the necessary information as well as did physical confirmation of the work in progress (WIP).

Physical progress (%)

	Materials on site	Machine shop	Ready for lift	Lift and welded	% Completed
Block 1	100	100	100	100	100
Block 2	100	100	100	100	100
Block 3	100	100	100	50	88
Block 4	100	75	0	0	44
Block 5	100	50	0	0	38
Block 6	100	50	0	0	38
Block 7	100	50	0	0	38
Block 8	100	25	0	0	31
Block 9	100	0	0	0	25
Block 10	100	0	0	0	25
				Average block progress	53
				Total project progress	11

Figure 2: Physical progress tracking (%)

Figure 2 is a sample of the different shipyard work areas tracked. The shipyard had a very detailed listing of each process step, and so this was used to monitor progress per step to understanding the actual progress. Also, this information was used when time came for progress payments as it would show total project completion. The monitoring of progress throughout the program allowed us to negotiate the next payment, depending upon the actual progress of the project. The budget for the steel work part of the project was 40 million dollars, so if a progress payment was due on this date, then no >4.2 million dollars should be paid out.

Time to complete in days

	Materials on site	Machine shop	Ready for lift	Lift and welded	Days completed
Block 1	0	5	1	2	8
Block 2	0	7	1	1	9
Block 3	0	7	1	1	9
Block 4	0	0	0	0	0
Block 5	0	0	0	0	0
Block 6	0	0	0	0	0
Block 7	0	0	0	0	0
Block 8	0	0	0	0	0
Block 9	0	0	0	0	0
Block 10	0	0	0	0	0

Average Block		8.67
Projected completion	433.33	
Promised completion	365	
Early/(Late) days		(68.33)

Figure 3: Actual time to complete each block assembly

Figure 3 is a recreation of the tracking that we were doing as part of the project. In this case, we were calculating the time that each block took to complete to forecast better at the end of the project. In this example, one can already see that each block is taking 8.67 days and so the forecasted completion would be over 2 months late. The shipyard was unwilling to accept the reality and made assurances that as the project continued that there would be an improvement. However, we were unconvinced and started to track one more metrics to show exactly where the problem was.

Rework time (days)

	Welding rework	Other rework	Total rework time
Block 1	0.5	0.25	0.75
Block 2	0.5	0	0.5
		Days lost	1.25

Figure 4: Rework time

The project team set about to determine the cause of the delay. The project team examined several variables, but one of the largest reasons for the project being behind schedule was the need for much rework, primarily welding work. As one can imagine, the weld seams on a vessel are what is holding the entire structure together, and so a poor weld will eventually fail or become a potential area of rust and weakens. There are specific requirements by class where welds must be completed in a particular manner to ensure structural integrity (American Bureau of Shipping, n.d.). There was an alarming trend for more and more rework as the shipyard would try to force their workers to speed up. A proper weld takes time and if one is not taking the time to make the weld correctly, then the inspector will likely see it and require rework. In other cases, inexperienced or new welders would take longer to complete a good weld and so speeding up those individuals only increased the error rate.

Figure 4 is a good example of helping the project team to research what was happening in the project. When the project team examined all the steps, it turned out that the welding workshop was often a problem area with the steelwork throughout the project. Inspectors would find problems with welds and there would be necessary rework. Also, the shipyard was short on experienced welders due to other projects, and so they would often get pulled elsewhere. The tracking of the metric on rework was important in documenting the delay of the shipyard. Identifying and documenting the problem allows the project team to show responsibility for the delay as penalty clauses could only be charged with documented proof.

Summary

In closing, this project offered some key learnings regarding metrics use in a project. These example metrics helped the project team explain and so the program manager could justify the use of penalty clauses in the project. Without this kind of documentation and detailed root- cause analysis, it is likely that less compensation for the delay would have occurred. It is clear that a project manager must always document and track progress, even when gathering the information might be challenging.

Chapter Twelve—Discussion/Quiz Questions

a. What is a metric?

b. Why is it important to a program?

c. Why should there be a clear way to monitor the progress of a program or project?

d. Should a program manager develop a custom monitoring process?

e. Can a monitoring progress anticipate future delays?

f. Should a program manager rely upon a monitoring metric?

g. Can increased production result in increased errors?

h. Can delays be avoided by using different metrics to track progress?

CHAPTER THIRTEEN
INTER-RELATIONSHIP OF PROGRAM MANAGEMENT AND REVERSE LOGISTICS

The reverse supply chain is the study of what happens to products, materials, or items after being sold to a client. Blanchard (2010) defines the reverse supply chain (reverse logistics) to be the process of moving goods from the consumer to capture value. The elements of the reverse supply chain that can have an impact at the program level includes returns, recalls, and salvage of the goods including any reuse of the packaging or shipping materials (Blanchard, 2010). In this chapter, the discussion will focus on the area of electronics because almost every program will have some form of computers and/or electronics that can be reused or recycled by the end of the program.

The reverse logistics at the program level have several important areas to consider such as returns, recalls, and recycling. The transportation of electronics gets completed by truck, rail, air, or sea. In many cases, electronics will move from the point of manufacturing via intermodal freight because products of this type will often originate outside of the United States and then move throughout the United States. Although there are many forms of logistics available with regard to the logistics of electronics, there are often far fewer options when one is working with the reverse supply chain of electronics. Most of these reverse supply chain transactions with electronics will start with the customer interacting with some customer service group associated with the electronics company.

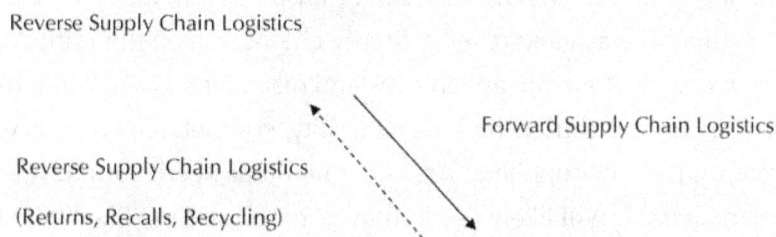

Reverse Supply Chain Logistics

Forward Supply Chain Logistics

Reverse Supply Chain Logistics

(Returns, Recalls, Recycling)

Figure 5: Forward and reverse logistics

To understand reverse supply chain logistics, one needs to understand some of the complexities of forward supply chain logistics (Figure 5). The creation of complex electronics requires engineering and manufacturing expertise; however, it also requires many logistics. All of the materials not made by the company will need to come from somewhere else and arrive, when needed, at the manufacturing company. Once all of that is completed, the finished goods require worldwide distribution. The products can then be sold in retail outlets. However, supply chain logistics originates with the customer and that customer needs to be able to get their product back to individuals that will exchange, repair, or recycle the product. Unlike large electronic firms that hire specialists with experience in logistics, a typical household will lack any expertise. Also, the original packaging that was meticulously developed to transport the product safely will have likely been thrown away by the consumer. The burden of packing and shipping rests upon the customer, who only wants his product repaired as quickly as possible.

Modes of Transportation

With regard to reverse supply chain logistics, there are two most common forms of transportation. First comes motor carrier (including small parcel delivery) and the second being air freight (including small parcel delivery). Motor carriers offer the most flexible means of overland transportation. In general, motor carrier transportation is the most common means of transportation. Trucks deliver the majority of items to individuals in the United States. The reverse supply chain is no different as the most common form of return or recall item will ship back to the manufacturer or their designee by truck. The product might go to a product depot for repair, or it may just be consolidated and shipped by to the manufacturer by sea.

There are some shortcomings with motor carrier transportation; motor carriers are a significant part of both the forward and reverse supply chains. Given the importance of motor carriers in supply chains, there are advantages and disadvantages to using motor carriers. Advantages to using motor carriers include flexibility, competitive rates, as well as having several different options for suppliers. An individual that needs to return a product to a company or manufacturer will likely use a small parcel company like UPS or FEDEX. The reason for this is the motor carriers can handle all shapes and sizes of materials as well as to handle all different types of material. Also, many of these small parcel delivery companies will also handle specialized packing, which electronics will likely need.

Disadvantages to using motor carriers include speed and cost. Air freight is much faster but does come at a much higher cost. Motor carriers can take up to a week to travel from one coast to the other in the United States while air carriers can deliver materials overnight. However, this cost element is a factor in the reverse supply chain because the company, not the consumer will likely have to pay the freight. If there is no more profit to be made on the transaction, it is in the best interest of the company to use the cheapest available transportation.

Air carriers and full-service air carriers such as UPS Air and FEDEX Overnight can address time; however, there will be an additional cost. The primary advantage is the speed of delivery; however, as this means that the cost of this freight will impact the profit of the sale, there needs to be a balance between the two. In many cases, there is often a 2 week period for returns to be processed and returned to the customer, even though the customer knows that they could pick up the phone and can order a new item that will be there the next day (Apple, n.d.).

Air carriers are reliable options for freight when the importance of time is the most significant aspect of the transaction. Motor carriers are the likely option when the cost is the most significant aspect of the transaction. In the end, air freight is one of the most expensive manners to move cargo; however, it is one of the fastest ways to move product from one place to another. Motor carriers offer a lower cost option that is slower in reaching the final destination of delivery.

Returns

Although customer services start in the buying and selling process of electronics, many customers are evaluating the customer service. Many people are very loyal to the brand of electronics that they purchase and often time's customers will purchase replacement units when they are available, rather than when they need a replacement. Because of this, many customers are interested in the handling of returns. If a new product does not meet the expectation, the customer wants to know what can be done to remedy the situation. In many retail organizations, the returns department is at the front of the store so one will get a firsthand look at the returns process. Never forget that people are watching because they are interested in what they may expect in the future. People want to have the entire experience completed as efficiently as the sales side. If the sales side is less than stellar, then the reverse supply chain needs to be even better to retain the person as a long-term customer.

Recalls

Although retailers do not like to believe that their extensively engineered and tested products are defective, every company that is in manufacturing or production long enough will experience a product recall. A product recall is often one of the most complex challenges of reverse supply chain logistics. A recall involves the mass return of a product that has been established to be in some way defective in a manner that the customer cannot correct safely or economically. A recall requires complex transportation requirements as products need to get from the customer to the manufacturer for replacement or correction. The product recall is often a public relations issue as well because of the intense media coverage that a product recall can get. The product recall is also the most sensational aspect of reverse supply chain logistics because it is precisely this scenario that differentiates the successful supply chain companies from the less successful supply chain companies.

Improperly managed product recalls have had significant impacts on organizations due to the media frenzy that develops when issues linger and consumers get injured. Recently, Toyota was under significant scrutiny by the U.S. government due to known product issues that were being knowingly or unknowingly ignored (Atiyeh & Blackwell, 2016). This intervention and the media coverage that followed tarnished the reputation of Toyota and Takata to the point that all of their quality was under scrutiny (US Government, 2015). A better mechanism to handle a product recall could have saved this company considerable loss of market share as American buyers moved on to other brands.

Recycling

Electronics recycling has become more sophisticated over the years, and some companies have made it a customer service priority like Best Buy. For years, Best Buy has been encouraging recycling of electronics by offering free recycling for all consumer electronics. Only recently, they have started to charge for this service (Bishop, 2016). It appears that consumers were happy to bring electronics for recycling and Best Buy were willing to handle the recycling, but it appears that the freight and handling costs were becoming too high. Offering recycling brings customers in to look when they are done with some electronics (Bishop, 2016). Best Buy knows that additional foot traffic to a retail store leads to greater sales. A person coming to return an item might find something that they want and that kind of foot traffic is essential for a retail store. It is a fact that such a large retail chain is handling the transportation and logistics or electronic recycling on a massive scale shows an interest in the company in operating as green as possible. The fact that there has been so much interest generated by customers that Best Buy feels it can, at least, mitigate the loss is a clear indication that the public is interested in a company staying green.

Another example in the electronics industry is that Apple, as well as most major cell phone providers, will now purchase back old equipment (Apple, n.d.). This kind of buy-back or used purchase is typical for the secondary market; however, it could also be for recycling. The choice to resell or recycle would depend on how old the technology is and how much demand there is for older equipment.

Also, the Resource Conservation and Recovery Act (RCRA) require that government agencies and government employees follow specific guidelines about recycling (GSA, 2015). The RCRA has made more government agencies accountable to recycle and take appropriate measure to reduce waste whenever possible. Furthermore, the GSA will offer assistance to allow all government buildings and offices to be more environmentally oriented (GSA, 2015).

Summary

In conclusion, the modes of freight and the elements of returns, recalls, and recycling cannot be ignored. These elements have a strong impact on the reverse supply chain and have an impact on the bottom line of any organization. Organizations that are successful in the transportation and logistics side of the reverse supply chain will be more successful than those that ignore this important strategy.

Chapter Thirteen—Discussion/Quiz Questions

a. What is reverse logistics at the program level?

b. Why are returns, recalls, and salvage important at the program level?

c. Why is the return of finished goods than the return of damaged goods?

d. Why is packing important?

e. What are modes of transportation?

f. How are modes of transportation important to reverse logistics?

g. Are motor carriers always the best choice?

h. What are some of the strengths and weaknesses of using a small parcel carrier?

i. What is the most expensive form of freight?

j. Are all air carriers the same?

k. What differentiates a full-service air carrier from other carriers?

l. What form of freight is used most often for returns?

m. What can happen if a recall is handled poorly?

n. What are the risks of delaying a recall?

o. Can recycling increase retail business?

p. Should one consider a buyback program for surplus material(s)?

CHAPTER FOURTEEN
SUMMARY

"A project manager can delegate authority but not responsibility. Responsibility is indivisible. When something goes wrong, and you cannot find the specific individual to put your finger on, then you have never really had the responsibility."

Hyman J. Rickover
Admiral, U.S. Navy (retired)
The New York Times, October 7, 1963

This quote from Admiral Rickover serves to illustrate an important fact about project and program management. Business today is more dynamic, and project managers must be very flexible to meet their client's needs. Clients are demanding greater results from fewer individuals in a shorter amount of time. A great project manager can always deliver exceptional results, even in the most difficult of projects. Great project managers help build a successful program. A program cannot be successful without having many successful project managers.

Project managers are increasingly being tasked with implementing change at all levels in all organizations. The role of project manager has become incredibly challenging due to the complexity of assignments (Curlee & Gordon, 2010). Because all business assignments are leadership assignments and can be made into projects, all managers must learn to master project leadership. Projects, especially the completed ones, allow individuals to showcase their talents to others in their company and others in their industry. Project managers and program managers have five similar strategies that can make them both successful. To combine these roles, in this section there will be a reference to the PL, which is both the project manager and the program manager. Given the similarities in the roles, there are five strategies that all successful PLs share. The five strategies are vision, authority, planning, speed, and contingency.

The first strategy of the PL is vision. A PL must have a clear picture of the final result. It is critical to have this vision before any progress toward the goal. The PL must be able to imagine in vivid detail all aspects of the completed project. The learning here is that no one person will ever complete a project alone. Learn to enlist the aid of everyone directly or indirectly involved. The better one can communicate the project vision, the better one will be able to mobilize other individuals. To have others participate fully in the project, these other people must be able to visualize the desired result. Explain all of the concepts to others to be sure they fully comprehend the vision. Everyone must have a clear vision of the goal; otherwise, everyone will not be able to move in harmony toward the goal. The vision must be clear; a vision with complicated metaphors is not useful. The project vision must be articulated at every opportunity to maintain enthusiasm and support. Practice being the vision of the project, and practice this strategy at every opportunity.

Authority is the second most important strategy. The PL must have the final authority to make decisions regarding the project. The PL's decision must be final, and he must have full authorization from the powers to complete the project or program. Less seasoned individuals may accept a project without having full authority. A PL without authority is at a serious disadvantage, and this situation is to be avoided at all costs. If an individual accepts a project without full authority, then the most probable outcome is a failure. The PL must always own all aspects of the project; then it would be best to withdraw from a project. When declining or withdrawing from a project, always explain one's unwillingness to accept the project is due to the lack of authority. Although it may be difficult to reject or withdraw from the project or program at the time, it will build the credibility of the PL, especially if it turns out that the project failed just as anticipated. Keep in mind the same holds true when a new project is offered without full authority, the same withdrawal or rejection applies. If at all possible, do not accept the project. Accepting a role with less than full authority is a critical mistake made by less experienced managers. Avoid this trap.

Planning the path is the third successful strategy. Successful projects never happen on time and budget by accident. Always spend considerable time planning in advance to organize every dimension of a project. All projects must have a beginning, middle, and an end. All successful projects and programs must follow a pre-established path that eventually concludes with the desired result. No one would ever jump into a car and start driving to a new destination without consulting others for directions or reviewing a map. Despite this obvious statement, many project managers proceed in just this manner. Less successful individuals move forward in a direction without giving the path that will be traveled any consideration. Planning means giving thought to the path and the destination. Planning becomes the road map to success. Structured planning serves to organize thoughts and task, while also illustrating, and directing all individuals toward the ultimate goal. A PL must always have a timeline to monitor progress. Monitoring progress is the only way to keep from falling behind schedule. All projects move forward through a series of tasks being completed. By monitoring the progress of tasks, the successful P.L. will know where the project is along the path at all times.

The fourth strategy is speed. The truly memorable projects are always the ones that were completed in the shortest amount of time. Appreciate and understand the need for speed. There will be situations when tasks need to be completed swiftly to meet deadlines. Those who fail to master the quagmire of politics within an organization will fail. Those individuals who are easily paralyzed by analysis or committees are doomed. More projects have failed due to politics or committees than by any other reason. Learn to leverage all resources, regardless if they are directly involved with that project or not. Greatness as a PL comes from having a group of individuals performs tasks that are completed to the delight of the client, regardless of the circumstances. All projects will have crunch times, where a lucky few will be forced to complete much more than originally envisioned. It is at these times in the project or program where the true value of speed will be realized by the PL.

Contingency is the fifth and final program management strategy. Plan and prepare for the unexpected are the mantras of the successful project manager. Create a plan to cover potential circumstances that might occur. No project will progress exactly according to the original schedule. The PL must be ready to adapt to unforeseen circumstances. There are always alternatives to any problem; it is just a matter of identifying them before making a decision. Remember, just because a solution handles the problem does not mean that it is the only solution. Sometimes it is better to prepare a complete contingency of alternates and keep this list available during the project rather than trying to solve problems when under time pressure. The PL should always consider the worst case scenario and determine a plan to cope with those situations. This preplanning will serve to handle these potential circumstances if they arise rather than falling victim to project paralysis. Anyone can steer a ship when the seas are calm, but it takes an exceptional master to keep a ship steady when the seas are rough.

Thus, all of these strategies are important for success. One must continually focus on the goal and travel as close to the planned path as possible. Focus and determination are principle attributes that lead to success. All projects when they are close to completion appear as if they will not finish on time. The PL must rise above these circumstances and remain focused on the task at hand. To waver in the face of challenges has dramatic effects on a project. When a leader loses his resolve, one can be sure that others on the project will lose focus. Never lose sight that the goal is to complete the project to the highest possible standards. Success or failure of the project always rests in the hands of the leaders. Following these strategies alone will not guarantee success; however, ignoring these strategies will certainly contribute to the failure of any project.

Chapter Fourteen—Discussion/Quiz Questions

    a. Is project leadership important? Why or why not?

    b. What makes a good PL?

    c. Should a PL communicate the goal of the project to others? Why or why not?

    d. Does a PL need to have vision?

    e. Should a leader have authority? Why or why not?

    f. Is planning important to leadership?

    g. Why is speed an important element of leadership?

    h. Why are having contingencies important to leadership?

    i. Does leadership drive success or failure? Why or why not?

SECTION FOUR
PORTFOLIO MANAGEMENT PERSPECTIVES

CHAPTER FIFTEEN
INTER-RELATIONSHIP OF PORTFOLIO MANAGEMENT AND CONTRACTING AND ACQUISITION

An important aspect of contract and acquisition that relates to portfolio management consists of the operational manufacturing, planning, control, and the financial understanding of the time value of money. In a portfolio of projects, there will be some level of manufacturing that will be required to support the various elements of different projects. To this end, understanding control and demand can ensure that all projects in the portfolio receive the necessary manufacturing support for success. Goods will either be make-to-stock, assemble-to-order, make-to-order, or full customization; however, in each of these cases one must consider the financial implications.

Manufacturing, planning, and control (MPC) are defined by the customer order decoupling point, which is the point that the demand goes from being independent to dependent (Jacobs, Berry, Whybark, & Vollman, 2011). MPC can happen in different environments such as make-to-stock, assemble-to-order, make-to-order, or full customization (Jacobs et al., 2011). Each of these is very distinct and has a different decoupling point, planning point, and control point.

First, in the make-to-stock environment, the decoupling point happens when the materials transition to completed goods. When the product is WIP and before, all items are considered dependent upon the finished product (Boyer & Verma, 2010). One can imagine this in a fast food restaurant where food is premade in advance of a lunch rush. The ingredients are independent of demand and need to be managed based on the expectation of the amount of finished goods to be made available. In this example, the kitchen would need to prep all the materials needed to meet a projected number of finished goods.

Planning for the make-to-stock environment would come from the forecast that would be used to project inventory levels. Control would come from customer feedback and stock outages or stock build up. If projections are off, then inventory would either grow or shrink.

Second, in the assemble-to-order environment, the goods remain independent until they become WIP. Products are assembled based upon available parts which are then brought together to meet the need. An example of this would be the quick serve restaurant Chipotle. One can see all the ingredients available for the different menu items and the customer can request a specific assembly of these items. Once the customer orders and production starts, the items transition from independent to dependent. The WIP is when all the materials are put out on display and available to fulfill customer orders.

Planning for the assemble-to-order environment would come from configuration management (Blanchard, 2010). One would be able to review prior history to see what items had greater demand based upon the bill of materials for each item ordered. Again, inventory growth or shrinkage would also direct what materials need more frequent ordering.

Third, in the make-to-order environment, the goods remain independent only as long as they remain as raw materials. Items will be ordered for stock, and those goods are then available for the order. In the make-to-order environment, items might be ordered specifically for a customer such as seen with a custom cake order. A person might order a specific combination of cake, frosting, and filling and further require a special message written on the cake. A custom order results in purchasing special ingredients to fulfill the request. At Baskin Robbins, one can order a special custom ice cream cake with writing and other details for an event.

Planning for the make-to-order environment is driven by past orders and those orders specifications. Although one might not be able to project exact demand, one might see patterns of more popular requests and tailor a more appropriate response. Control comes from customer feedback as well as from how often the organization was able to meet customer deadlines.

Fourth, is full customization where someone might be able to order a fully customized item that would be unique. For example, someone could commission a wedding cake that was seven layers, with each layer being a different cake, filling, and frosting, as well as each layer having unique decorations. In this case, the decoupling point would be as soon as the items are ordered from vendors because there would be no other possible use for the materials except for that custom application.

Planning for the full customization environment is dependent upon specifications but given that there would be so many possibilities, in most cases demand could not be fore-casted, however, the organization can set up relationships where more common items arrive quickly. The organization might not be able to stock everything, but it should be able to create relationships with suppliers to be able to bring in most items quickly. Control comes from customer feedback as well as managing the customer relationship.

Fifth is understanding the value of money in business. The value of money is a complex matter in business because the value of money changes over time. Although many are familiar with the concept of the time value of money, this concept is not always applied in business due to the short-term goals of an organization. However, with a capital project, one needs to consider the cost of money against the rate of return on the capital investment (Project Management Institute, 2008). For a project to move forward, it requires that the ROI be more than the opportunity costs associated with the project. If the return is too low, then it is better to use that money for another purpose. Furthermore, the ROI needs to overcome the opportunity cost of the money as well as the loss of purchasing power of money in the future.

The capital involved in a portfolio of projects should offer tangible benefits that result in some long-term return. For example, the construction of a group of office buildings should result in a tangible financial return over the life of each of the buildings. If the long-term return does not overcome the costs to build the office building, then there would be great difficulty in getting the project approved. If the costs were higher than the return unless there are other mitigating circumstances, the project would be a "no-go." Of course, there are times where there are long-term strategic goals achieved by a capital project, such as increasing market share or because of governmental subsidies.

In addition to the long-term return, a capital project would have to show that the money spent today would be less than money spent in the future. If this hurdle is not achieved, then the project might be delayed until such time where the money spent today is less than the money spent in the future. For example, it is accepted that the money of today is worth more than the money in the future. The reason for this important calculation is because money today can be invested and that money will compound interest over time and become more money. Also, we see the impact of inflation and rising costs for more material items. So, an important factor in the "go–no go" decision is to determine if the money spent today is less than money spent in the future.

This time value of money calculation is very important for a capital project due to the temporal nature of the project that might take years to complete. With an investment that might take years before it generates revenue makes the discussion about the costs quite relevant. Ultimately, the time value of money would need to be calculated for any capital type project that would take a long period to complete as well as a long period to depreciate. This understanding of the time value of money will impact any "go or no go" decision for a project because if the value does not overcome this hurdle, then it is better to use the money for a different investment.

Summary

In conclusion, the operational decoupling point is different in each of these environments. Also, each environment operates with different controls and planning systems. Also, the impact of the cost of capital cannot be forgotten, regardless of the operational benefit. The portfolio manager must consider and balance both the operational benefits against the cost of the capital being invested in the portfolio. If there are no benefits in both areas, the portfolio manager should re-examine each of the projects to make sure that all of them make sense to complete.

Chapter Fifteen—Discussion/Quiz Questions

a. Why is manufacturing important in a portfolio?

b. Explain make-to-stock.

c. Explain assemble-to-order.

d. Explain make-to-order.

e. Explain full customization.

f. What is the time value of money?

g. What is ROI?

h. Why is long-term return important for a portfolio?

i. Is money today the same as money in the future?

j. Should one always calculate the time value of money in any project, program or portfolio?

CHAPTER SIXTEEN
INTER-RELATIONSHIP OF PORTFOLIO MANAGEMENT AND TRANSPORTATION AND LOGISTICS

Portfolio management often requires taking a big picture view of all the projects involved. In many cases, this means being able to adjust to the changing demands of customers and suppliers. Organizations start out with a plan to address the expected challenges. However, the unexpected challenges often cause the largest issues for the projects in a portfolio. Given that there could be several projects in a portfolio, the potential for issues grows exponentially. As such, portfolio managers involved with transportation and logistics should be aware of air carriers and production schedules. Air carriers can arrange for delivery of goods faster than other freight options and become familiar with production schedules which can help better understand how products are being manufactured and potentially being delayed.

Full-Service Air Carriers

The most likely air carrier type that would be used to expedite goods would be a full-service air carrier. Using a full-service air career can eliminate many of the concerns regarding shipping. One can look at the relationship between an organization like Amazon.com and UPS. Amazon.com has a lot at stake with utilizing air carriers because Amazon.com customers are paying for a service (freight) and customers will hold Amazon.com accountable for the actions or inactions of the air carrier. The portfolio manager and the client(s) will also have such a relationship as the portfolio manager will be held accountable for delays, even when those delays might have been out of the direct control of the portfolio manager. As such, there are many advantages to using a full-service air carrier, but there are also some disadvantages to using a full-service air carrier, so a portfolio manager should be aware of the potential of full-service air carriers.

Two advantages of using a full-service carrier are the potential for bundling freight as well as the advantage of speed. With the example used earlier where Amazon.com is working with UPS, one considerable advantage for Amazon.com is that they can negotiate a better freight rate for all the services UPS is providing. Although air does cost more than surface freight, the overall cost of freight can be reduced when one bundles all the services of the full-service air carrier. This economy of scale can be a significant example when it comes to controlling costs.

Air freight also has the advantage of speed. A full-service air carrier can work with the aviation authorities to ensure arrival and departure times occur on schedule and so the choice of the air carrier can be very important to the success of the delivery of the freight.

A significant disadvantage of a full-service air carrier is cost. A full-service air carrier will cost significantly more than surface freight, and so the commodity being shipped must be important enough to consider this option. Keep in mind that the importance is the perception of the customer, not the perception of the air carrier.

In closing, air carriers are reliable options for freight and can be considered when the importance of time is significant to the client. In the end, air freight is one of the most expensive manners to move cargo. However, it is one of the fastest ways to move product from one place to another.

Production Strategies

There are three production strategies as well as master production scheduling and stability time fencing. The three production strategies are chase production, level production, and mixed combination production. The freeze concept will be discussed, and how it relates to master production schedule stability time fencing. The freeze concept will be applied to the manufacturing of bicycles. All of these strategies offer insights to manufacturing production. However, these concepts also apply to various service industries as well.

Chase production strategy is where the organization adjusts capacity to match the demand pattern (Wisner et al., 2012). In many manufacturing companies, they would cease production during certain summer months due to being able to produce earlier in the year the products needed for the most of the remainder of the year. This summer closure could be adjusted to be longer or shorter to meet the demand of the product. An example of this in logistics happens with UPS, where during the holiday season where there is a huge rise in the movement of packages, UPS will hire seasonal employees to meet the high demand for logistics at the end of the year.

Level production strategy relies on a level output rate and increases in demand are addressed through the use of built up inventory (Wisner et al., 2012). For example, an oil well will produce at a consistent rate and flow for most of its useful life. During that period, production will remain level regardless of seasonal factors. This level production exists in the logistics with the U.S. Mail service. Mail moves year round and is delivered on 6 days a week, regardless of seasonal usage. Mail moves slower during seasonal periods and faster during off-peak times.

Mixed combination production strategy combines level and chase production strategies by maintaining a core group that can flex with the demands and needs of the market (Wisner et al., 2012). Using a mixed combination production strategy means that an organization might grow to a certain size to accommodate the core group and then it might lease additional space or equipment only when necessary due to increased demand. This strategy also implies that the organization would not be in the habit of building up inventories. The organization would typically be manufacturing to meet either the expected low demand or perhaps units are built to order. There is a mixed combination production strategy with regard to Starbucks coffee shops. It is not possible to build up an inventory of lattes and so the coffee shop will be built to accommodate the usual demand and might bring on additional people during peak periods. The purchase of raw materials(coffee beans and milk, for example) and additional people can be used to help expedite and keep up with demand. The mixed combination production strategy is the demand strategy used by a third-party logistics company (3PL). A 3PL might have a core group of truckers, but it utilizes independent truckers when there is additional work available. A 3PL can be utilized to maintain a core of full-time truckers but it can flex to meet the periods of greater demand.

Master production scheduling is a detailed, time-restricted view of production (Wisner et al., 2012). In manufacturing, master production might be broken down into the components that make up the final product. This way there is an understanding of the demand for each component and each component can be scheduled sequentially to allow smooth production of the required items to meet the demand.

In the manufacturing of bicycles, one can envision the manufacturing of each component of the bicycle so that the final assembly can come together. One might be able to build the frame, wheels, and handlebars in parallel, but frames are needed first because, without a frame, the wheels and handlebars will have to wait for assembly. As one can see from this example, master production scheduling is highly dependent upon different time buckets (Wisner et al., 2012).

In the service industry, one can visualize the master production schedule as the appointment book for required work (Boyer & Verma, 2010). The appointment book or one might see this as the role of a trucking dispatcher where the daily deliveries, but it requires planning, routing, and loading of each truck to achieve the most efficient deliveries. Scheduled deliveries should not strain capacity while still meeting the expectations of customers.

To address the challenges of master production scheduling, many organizations utilize the concept of a master production scheduling time fence. A master production scheduling time fence addresses the difference between firm demand and anticipated demand. This concept is an extension of the freeze concept because this helps address the challenges of a frozen schedule where it becomes difficult to change the direction of production once it has begun to move forward (Jacobs et al., 2011).

Think of a time fence as the difference between the manufacturing of bicycles with actual orders as opposed to anticipated demand. The master production time fence requires that senior management approves a change the current period production for actual orders. The planning time fence for anticipated demand allows production for a later period and can be changed to meet the needs of the organization (Jacobs et al., 2011).

In conclusion, there are many ways to schedule and many ways to meet the demands of the supply chain (Blanchard, 2010). An organization determines what is in their best interest and spends time modifying the process to improve the utilization of labor and capital. Organizations that understand that demand planning might need to change from year to year to better achieve the results of the organization. In many cases, this means to change earlier to meet the expected demand. In prior years unexpected demand caused FEDEX and UPS delivery drivers to continue delivery on Christmas to meet the expectations of customers.

Chapter Sixteen—Discussion/Quiz Questions

a. Does portfolio management require a big picture view regarding all the projects?

b. What is the importance of full-service air carriers?

c. Why are full-service air carriers more likely to be part of a portfolio?

d. What are the advantages of a full-service air carrier?

e. What are the disadvantages of a full-service air carrier?

f. Why would the speed of product movement be important at the portfolio level?

g. What are production strategies?

h. Explain chase production.

i. Explain level production.

j. Explain mixed combination production.

k. Explain the importance of a time fence.

l. Why are production strategies important at the portfolio level?

CHAPTER SEVENTEEN
INTER-RELATIONSHIP OF PORTFOLIO MANAGEMENT AND REVERSE LOGISTICS

Portfolio management and reverse logistic are related based upon the understanding of input and output control. The needs of the portfolio are the inputs, and reverse logistics are some of the outputs. Consider that every project and program are going to generate a deliverable for a client. That deliverable will be a product, system, building, ship, automated system, or another valuable element that an organization can use to satisfy clients. Everything that is leftover that is not part of the deliverable becomes the outputs of reverse logistics. Managing the portfolio of leftover materials is critical to the long-term success of the portfolio because properly managed remaining materials can significantly improve the profitability of the portfolio.

Inputs–Outputs

Input	Output—Client	Output—Reverse Logistics
Labor		Excess overhead
Computers		Excess or damaged items
Cabling	*Integrated supply chain*	Any remaining material
Routers	*MRP system*	Excess or damaged items
Terminators		Excess or damaged items
Servers		Excess or damaged items

Figure 6: Integrated supply chain requirements

As per Figure 6, if one considers the desired output as the implementation of a new MRP system, then the input would be all of the elements required to develop and launch that system. A new system launch utilizes an input–output system with some control mechanism. The project will require some estimates based on user needs and the clients requirements. However, these original estimates will change during each project in a portfolio. As all these change, there will be excess material and labor that will be purchased but might not be used in the final iteration of the project. Given that there are several projects in a portfolio, excess materials can start to grow.

When reviewing the inputs of a typical project, one finds labor as one of the largest costs in the project. The planning for this input can be quite complex as one needs to make sure that the labor is available to meet the demands of the project. If sufficient personnel are not available, then the project will likely suffer from delays and disruption. The organization should have controls and checks and balances to ensure that labor is available to meet the demand of the customers. In peak periods, this might mean having the extra personnel or having supplemental labor available. An organizational understanding of labor utilization can generate positive client satisfaction (Boyer & Verma, 2010).

Another major input is material. Computers, cables, routers, and servers are all materials that could be used during a system implementation. This input is particularly important as all these goods needs to be available, along with backup replacements to meet the demands of the operation. Imagine the chaos if there were not enough computer stations available for all employees. There would be considerable delays with training, and productivity would drop considerably.

A project might purchase massive quantities of these materials at once to garner a better price and to make sure that supplies arrive when required (Boyer & Verma, 2010). One possible consideration is to try to purchase all materials for different projects in a portfolio in bulk; however, this will require considerable timing and coordination to ensure that this is effective. Also, there needs to be a plan for what to do with any leftover materials. One good strategy is to develop a returns plan as part of the contract so that unused material can be returned. If that is not possible, one should consider using any leftover material for another project in the portfolio. Implementing a zero waste strategy can improve profitability and reduce the stockpiling of material in different warehouses.

Summary

In conclusion, the input–output strategy is necessary for portfolio management as it offers some different examples of capacity planning and control. Regardless of the operation, all organizations that apply reverse logistics strategies can become more profitable. Capacity planning is essential to an operation that depends on a lot of planning. If a project is not careful, the waste that it generates will pull down the profitability of the project. By better planning and use of products at the end of the project can improve profitability and improve the bottom line for the portfolio.

Chapter Seventeen—Discussion/Quiz Questions

a. Explain input control.

b. Explain output control.

c. Will there always be excess material in a portfolio? Why or why not?

d. What is one of the largest costs in a typical project?

e. How should one manage materials in a portfolio?

f. Should resources be shared between projects in a portfolio? Why or why not?

g. Should a returns process be part of a contract? Why or why not?

CHAPTER EIGHTEEN
SUMMARY

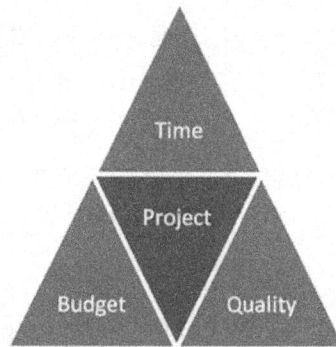

Figure 7: Triple restraints

The concept of triple restraints in project management is the belief that there are three competing forces on any project (Figure 7). There are requirements of time, budget, and quality, all which need to be organized by the project manager. In many cases, there is a relationship where increasing one will impact the other project restraints. Although this is often applied to project management, this same principle applies to portfolio management.

As a portfolio manager, one should be familiar with the high-level statement of work (SOW) of all the projects in the portfolio to determine the priority of the constraints of the client. In most cases, the element of time is the most critical aspect of the project (i.e., the client expects the project to be delivered on a specified date, by contract). However, there are times where time might not be the priority of the client, and then one needs to remain aware of budget and quality. There is a strong belief among project managers that an early delivery is a sign of success. However, this is something that might not be as important to the portfolio manager.

Early completion might not always be a positive because the client might not want the project done early. For example, completing a call center 1 month ahead of schedule might cause other complications and additional costs as the client needs to scramble to get other resources together. If the call center hardware and software is ready, but there are no people trained to use the equipment, this creates an expense as the asset will remain unused. Although the cost is the same to have space if the build out took longer, the perception will be that the project manager should have forecasted the completion date better to allow the client to manage their other resources. As such, this can have a huge impact on the portfolio if all the projects are being managed together.

Beyond this, it is important that relationship between the client, project manager, and the portfolio manager be clear from the start. This relationship will allow understanding of the project as the scope begins to drift from the original SOW. For example, if one were to increase the level of quality for a project, such as increasing redundancy, then one would expect a change in budget and a possible delay in delivery as new hardware needs to be specified and sourced.

Another example would be if the client wanted to reduce the budget, then one would expect that the project would be scaled down resulting in a reduction in the budget and also in quality. However, reducing the scope does not always improve the time because now the entire project needs to be reviewed with the scaled down specifications to determine other possible impacts. Just because one is now sourcing smaller servers does not mean that smaller servers are more readily available.

Ultimately, the project manager needs to monitor the project to determine the impact of these constraints, while keeping the portfolio manager up to date with changes as well. A good control mechanism is to use a robust change order system that documents all the changes in the project from the beginning. Many projects have failed due to scope creep, so one needs to make sure to manage all changes when they arise. Good control allows the project manager to keep the client updated on progress as well as changes to the schedule. Keeping the client updated on progress throughout the progress can avoid making the client upset about an early delivery or a late delivery. Keeping the portfolio manager updated on progress can avoid impacting other projects that are part of the portfolio.

Chapter Eighteen—Discussion/Quiz Questions

a. What are the triple restraints?

b. Explain the concept of triple restraints.

c. How important is time to a portfolio or project?

d. How important is budget to a portfolio or project?

e. How important is quality to a portfolio or project?

f. Is early completion always a positive?

g. When can early completion in a portfolio become an issue?

h. If one reduces one of the triple restrains, will the others increase? Why or why not?

i. What is a change order mechanism?

j. Why is change order management important to a project or portfolio?

SECTION FIVE
ETHICS AND CULTURAL PERSPECTIVES

CHAPTER NINETEEN
ETHICS AND CULTURE IN MODERN PROJECT, PROGRAM, AND PORTFOLIO MANAGEMENT

Project communication management is important to the success of any project, program, or portfolio. A project manager should have regular communication with their team, their client, and all their stakeholders. A project manager should divide their time in a way that they are in communication with their project stakeholders while remaining in touch with the progress of the project. Although a project manager has the choice of many forms of management and communication, the project manager should learn to be able to manage project team trust. If the project manager cannot manage the level of trust within the project, the project manager will never have a successful project. To this end, understanding trust and learning how to manage trust in a project become critical to success.

Trust is critical to project success, and project managers need to understand how to maintain trust within a project. Without trust, the project manager will struggle with the project, program, or portfolio success. In this regard, the examination of different types of trust is essential to offer the best practices in managing team trust. It is proposed to review three categories of trust, to better understand how and when these types of trust are most appropriate.

Wong (2007) describes three categories of trust: cognitive-based, system-based, and affect-based. Cognitive-based trust is the common form of trust that develops over time while working in proximity to one another. System-based trust consists of formal relationships such as found in contracts. Affect-based trust is an emotional trust developed from emotions and feelings. A review of each type of trust as well as how different types of trust can apply to a project will support the conclusions. In support of these discussions, an examination of these different types of trust has been done in various peer-reviewed journal articles. This examination regarding trust in projects, programs, and portfolios will establish support for best practices surrounding the building of trust.

The discussion in this chapter will establish which one out of the three types of trust identified has the greatest connection to project success. Although this research will be limited in scope, the goal is to offer an indication to what area(s) a project manager should focus upon regarding project, program, and portfolio communication. If a project manager can better understand trust, this could offer a project manager a time management technique that could assist them in future success. Being able to manage the amount of time spent on communication can make a difference between success and failure.

Cognitive-Based Trust

Cognitive-based trust comes from an early childhood concept. "Stranger danger" is a concept taught to children who are young and unable to identify the good people from the bad people rationally. In this context, this kind of teaching is hard to unlearn, and many people associate unknown people as untrustworthy. However, this concept does fade over time as people associate with one another. Once a person learns more about another person, they tend to see them as individuals rather than as unknown strangers.

So, to build up cognitive-based trust, an individual needs a difficult project commodity:-time. Solid relationships take time and although hierarchically people should respond to business objectives, there is a difference between working and thinking. People who trust one another will think of creative solutions to benefit the group. People who do not trust one another will just do the task put before them. Productivity and success come from people thinking to resolve situations and achieve goals, not by just moving their hands to appear busy.

Building cognitive-based trust is often in the hands of the project manager. If the project manager can make calls to get status updates, the project manager should spend the time to build a trusting relationship with the project team. Trust is earned by actions so the project manager should consider what actions he can take to earn the trust of others. Beyond this, the project manager should consider his actions to retain the trust of the team (Duarte & Sndyer, 2006). Trust is a requirement of the project because the nature of relationships will often determine success or failure of a project.

A good project manager creates trusting moments every day with the team. Just calling to get an update is not building trust, and in some cases, it is building resentment. Use the time for a status update to gather more information about the individual, their contribution as well as where they need help. Jack Welsh, GE's famous CEO, at one time, installed a phone that anyone in the company could call to speak directly to him about any cost-savings initiative that was working within the company. He wanted to create trust, and he wanted to hear from all levels of the organization. By creating this "hot line," Welsh learned more about what was going on the company than from any executive project status meeting.

System-Based Trust

According to Wong (2007), "Processes are the tools, techniques, and procedures used to get work done" (p. 70). Hence, system-based trust is based on tools, techniques, and procedures. To start, one can examine a common tool used to build trust in any organization. The implementation of a common trust tool can build up trust over time between individuals. A project manager can make a difference with team members by creating a reserve of trust, sometimes called a trust balance sheet (Gustafsson, Smyth, Ganskau, & Arhippainen, 2010). The assumption is that one can store trust over time because of prior actions of the individuals. Over time, individuals involved in a project or the same organization will have enough knowledge of each other to respect one another. Trust is an integral part of a successful virtual team, and hence any tool that can build trust will be helpful in a project (Duarte & Snyder, 2006). A common aspect of trust is that we tend to trust those whom we know and distrust those whom we do not know. This personal knowledge of another person can be used as a tool when one creates more trust over time by doing the right things. Also, one can become credible by taking action when needed and by doing what one promises to do. These types of predictable actions create a social reserve of trust.

According to Wong (2007), this mutual trust can build up over time and can be a powerful force in a successful project. Knowing a person is integral to trust because we do not know strangers and hence, one cannot predict their behavior. In turn, one cannot build a trust bank with strangers because unknown individuals are inherently untrustworthy. Trust is not static as it can change with each passing moment, based upon the actions of the individuals involved. Also, there is a transactional nature of trust, which builds and maintains long-term trust in a project. "Trust is therefore conceptually dynamic, iteratively and implicitly negotiated in each relationship or set of relationships" (Gustafsson et al., 2010, p. 423).

Creating trust is a challenge in a project, program, or portfolio because many times these organizations are predominantly virtual. Virtual project teams lack visual cues from body language, making for a disconnected relationship. Many experts refer to this as the water cooler or break room interaction that does not exist virtually. Trust is a major component of a successful virtual team (Duarte & Snyder, 2006). Because of this, the leaders that display consistent values and identifiable boundaries are more likely to be successful. However, this can be challenging because teams tend to be a temporary relationship and short-lived and hence maintaining trust can be difficult (Duarte & Synder, 2006).

A team charter can go a long way to create acceptable norms and acceptable behavior that will help move a team toward success (Wong, 2007). A team charter and team goals can help to make people want to work together. Creating an atmosphere of cooperation and collaboration builds trust in an organization. If people are given responsibly and allowed to manage their work, then it gives them greater flexibility in achievement. However, freedom does not mean that people can slack off. There still needs to be checks and balances to ensure accountability. A successful project has no need for a micromanager asking for hourly updates.

A successful team needs a means of holding team members accountable for deadlines and deliverables. Holding team members accountable and management supporting the agreed upon team values becomes critical toward building a successful team (Wong, 2007). This trust can build confidence in the project, in the leader, and the organization (Gustafsson et al., 2010). Confidence in leadership is essential to a successful project. Hence, trust would be a building block for success.

One notable technique to build trust in a project is the celebration of milestone success. Success builds trust. When a project and project team is successful, suddenly fans materialize to enjoy the success. Just like people who win the lottery, they suddenly find themselves surrounded by people who also wish to enjoy the success. Suddenly, people will trust each other more to bask in the success of the moment. However, the project manager should understand that the failure then becomes the antithesis to trust. Failure will cause people to lose trust faster than almost any other factor. When a project starts to fail, people will distance themselves from the project (and the people). No one wants to associate with failure.

Procedures are a solid system for trust. Once people understand and recognize what they need to do and who handles what, there is clarity in the workplace. People dislike when there is murkiness in an organization because then the business owners are unrecognizable. Just like the tragedy of the commons, if no one person is responsible, then no one will care for the common things in a project. However, keep in mind that it is not necessary to have a single person to handle any process. Procedures only document the tasks of an organization. There are times when a group manages a process rather than by a single individual. Some processes require a design that addresses the needs of the virtual organization. For example, instead of the project manager being responsible, the project team can have a formalized system to manage major decisions. Every employee does not have a right to a veto, but the process should allow them input. Keep in mind that most processes should involve more than one person's input in the decision-making process.

Project complexity has an impact when it comes to procedures and process. The greater the complexity of the project, the greater the need for the project team to trust one another (Malik, McDermott, & Swan, 2007). There is no doubt that this is something that the project manager needs to pay attention to because of the nature of projects. Trust becomes important when the lines of the process blur, and team members are left to make decisions without the benefit of immediate management support. Project team members want to feel trusted to take the necessary risks to complete the project. If they have to wait for approval, the project will suffer from internal delays that will often lead to failure.

Affect-Based Trust

The affect-based trust will likely be the hardest to build in an organization. Project managers tend to be less emotional and tend to hide their feelings more than most. Also, building these kinds of relationships take much effort and time by the project manager and the project team. However, this kind of trust does build up over multiple projects. When a team or most of a team stays together through a couple of projects, then they get better at working together and so it becomes a more efficient project organization.

Affect-based trust is one of the strongest bonds within a project team because this kind of relationship happens over time and typically over multiple projects. When a team works together, it offers a clear understanding of the different roles and strengths of the individuals makes a difference. Teams that already have an understanding of the different personalities will move quickly to a high level of production. If there are few conflicts about communication, role understanding, or personality, it makes for a more efficient organization. One can get this from a very homogenous organization. However, most projects, programs, and portfolios will have globally dispersed individuals in multiple groups working together. For example, if one were to apply the Tuckman ladder (Forming—Storming—Norming—Performing—Adjourning), an experienced team can move quickly to the performing stage (Project Management Institute, 2013a). When people know one another, they can move quickly through the earlier stages that are more associated with conflict (Duarte & Snyder, 2006). This rapid movement to performing is less risky because people know what to expect from one another, unlike when people do not know each other, there is a greater risk of conflict. When people know what to expect from each other, then they are more likely to work out the problems than to allow it to build into a larger conflict. Additionally, when ground rules exist from prior interactions and projects, there are clear expectations, and this early commitment will decrease misunderstandings (Project Management Institute, 2103a).

Wong (2007) supports the notion that affect-based trust can be motivating as well as it can build a strong team. Wong's statement contrasts the impression given by the PMBOK. The PMBOK states very little practical information other than placing an importance on "soft skills" (Project Management Institute, 2013a). When a team is working successfully together, it will, in turn, generate more success. When one has the feeling of camaraderie and high esprit de corps, it can influence the perception of a project. If a team is cohesive and working together, it will cause anyone observing the team admire their perseverance. Great teams remain in the social memory for decades. The Miami Dolphins and their perfect season continue to be a source of pride for a football franchise that never seems to win football championships like other famous franchises. The "Miracle on Ice" team that beat the Soviet's during the Olympics at the height of the Cold War continues to show how great teams are admired long after their success has passed.

One often overlooked element of affect-based trust is honesty. Although one would assume that this would be a given, anyone involved with a large organization knows that politics will often be a factor. Also, any large project is going to be impacted by the politics of the project sponsor, the organization, and the client. According to data from project team members, honesty is an essential element for project trust and project success (Malik et al., 2007).

Best Practices Review

Given the presented information and research, it is now necessary to review the literature. A literature review will identify best practices in building trust, particularly in virtual IT projects. Given that the material reviewed had a direct or indirect focus upon trust, it is necessary to identify the overlapping concepts presented to come up with some ranking of the best practices discussed.

Figure 8 presents the top best practices in the literature regarding trust and project success. When an author is clear about their support of a given best practice, a "Yes" is entered in the table. If the author is silent or vague, the field is left blank. The results offer a view to the most prolific best practices in the reviewed literature.

	Trust takes time	Trust is	Shared	Trust balance	Success	Honesty
Carstea (2014)		Yes	Yes			
Duarte, Synder (2006)	Yes		Yes		Yes	
Gordon, Curlee (2011)	Yes	Yes	Yes	Yes	Yes	
Gustafsson, Smith, Ganskau, Arhippainen (2010)	Yes	Yes	Yes	Yes		Yes
Malik, Khalfan, Swan (2007)	Yes	Yes	Yes			Yes
PMBOK (2013a)	Yes		Yes			
Wong (2007)	Yes		Yes			

Figure 8: Best practices by author

A quick review of Figure 8 makes it very clear that the best practices regarding trust consist of trust taking time and the project team needs to have shared goals. Building trust takes time according to almost all the examined literature about trust. However, the shared goals concept needs a little additional explanation. Although the literature identified shared goals as a requirement of a successful team and team trust, just having shared goal on paper is not enough. It was clear that all of the authors believe that this was something that was in the realm of the leadership of the project manager. Meaning, just giving team members a shared goal checklist was meaningless if the project manager and the organization do not model and behaved congruently to the shared goals. It would appear obvious that a project would have a shared goal (finish the project). However, the communication and constant modeling of shared goals help make a project successful.

Summary

As more project managers rely on technology, building trust and good communication are becoming forgotten elements of a successful project. Virtual project managers should not lose sight of the basic building blocks of organizational success. There is no doubt that social skills are just as important, if not more important, than cost, scope, and schedule. The issue is that a project manager is taught to focus on cost, scope, and deadlines. However, just monitoring these elements does not ensure project success. Project managers forget that people determine the budget, quality, and deadlines. If there is no trust, there will be strife. Strife and conflict can lead to confusion in the best case and sabotage in the worst case.

People that share a common goal with leadership are people that have gotten to know one another over time. Because team building takes great effort, an experienced project manager will likely use the same individuals and resources for similar tasks. Even a finely tuned machine will fail without regular maintenance. Project managers fail to understand the importance of trust. Instead, they focus on results, and when results are not present, they may seek to place blame. In a large complex project the budgets, deadlines, and other situations can overwhelm the project manager. With so many external pressures upon the project manager, this often leaves no time to devote to the soft skills that the PMBOK identifies as so important. Research shows that one needs time to create trust in a project team. Trust comes in time, and there is no path to instant trust. There is no absolute method to create trust, but when a project manager focuses on communication, that emphasis will go a long way to building confidence (Malik et al., 2007).

Chapter Nineteen—Discussion/Quiz Questions

a. Is communication important?

b. Is trust part of communication?

c. Is trust important to project success?

d. According to Wong (2007), how many categories of trust are there?

e. Explain cognitive-based trust.

f. Explain system-based trust.

g. Explain affect-based trust.

h. Which category of trust is most important?

i. Which type of trust is associated with strangers or unknown parties?

j. Does cognitive-based trust need a lot of time to develop? Why or why not?

k. What is a team charter?

l. Can a team charter help build trust?

m. Does a celebration help build trust?

n. Do systems help build trust?

o. What can a portfolio manager do to build trust?

p. Do complex project help build or help tear down trust?

q. Is affect-based trust easy to create? Why or why not?

r. Can affect-based trust be motivating? Why or why not?

s. Is honesty and trust related? Why or why not?

CHAPTER TWENTY
ETHICS AND CULTURE IN CONTRACTING AND ACQUISITION

Although there are many ethical and cultural aspects in the field of government contracting and acquisition, one area of particular note is the area of drug testing in the workplace. It is a common requirement for government workers to be willing to take a company managed drug test to confirm that an employee is not using drugs. However, as different states are enacting laws allowing for the recreational use of drugs, this is becoming a greater challenge for government agencies. As drug testing is a requirement, there is growing concern regarding the rights of the employee in the workplace. Human Resource departments are increasingly under pressure to have a consistent screening policy for new employees to ensure hiring the best possible candidates. Coupled with this is the requirement that Human Resource departments apply consistent rules when confronted with the issue of drugs in the workplace. The moral question is as follows: Do employers have the right to test individuals in the workplace for drug use? Furthermore, does a company have a right to know about drug use of an individual if that drug use happened during their time off? This chapter will explore many layers of this issue. This process will evaluate the rights of an employee, the legal perspective, existing policies, and employee alternatives with regard to drug testing in the workplace.

Rights of an Employee

There is moral and legal obligation of an organization to an employee to offer a safe work environment and compensation for labor services provided. In return, the employee is morally bound to offer the best possible service for the employer, as well as loyalty to the firm. This relationship normally does not seem to cover drug testing in the workplace. However, both sides have taken positions regarding the issue of drug testing in the workplace.

Employers will take the position that a safe work environment is one free of drugs and drug users. Employers see drugs as a danger to individuals and the organization. Drugs can contribute to accidents and injuries. If this is true, then an organization should take the position that drug testing is an acceptable means of ensuring safety. Although this might be true, the reality is potentially more sinister and far reaching. Drug-testing technology can detect substances utilized up to 21 days prior (Beauchamp, 1997). Unlike alcohol that is absorbed by the body typically within a few hours, drugs can remain detectable in urine and blood for much longer. Drug testing can determine use. However, drug testing cannot determine exactly when the drugs were used. Drug testing can only find whether certain elements related to drug use are present. This timing issue creates for a deeper moral quagmire, as information regarding drug use could be potentially invasive information. Experts agree that being under the influence of drugs or alcohol can affect one's performance at the time. However, there is no proven data that recent drug use (within a few days or weeks) has any impact on job performance.

This timing issue brings rise to the harder question, does recent drug use attributed to accidents in the workplace? Does an employer have the right to invade the "off time" of the employee, when the use of certain drugs is allowed for recreational purposes by the state, under the guise of a safe work environment?

The employee can take the position that they are not compensated during their free time, and hence no loyalty exists during their time off. Work time is paid time, and hence drug testing is used to implicate drug use during one's free time is unjust. In the United States it is a crime to drive while under the influence of drugs. In fact, some states allow for recreational use of drugs or the medicinal use of certain otherwise "illegal" drugs for ill patients. Of course, use requires possession. However, drug testing in the workplace allows for discovery of usage without possession. Hence, this data about drug use could be used for other decisions, notably to employ or not to employ; however, this data does not have to be turned over to the authorities. Another area that is usually not examined is the right of consultants and suppliers. Although these individuals are not directly on the payroll, these individuals do contribute to the safety of the organization. Although it is argued that these individuals be only transitory and can be eliminated without cause, they still may be drug users contributing to a delinquent and unsafe work environment. Most companies fail to administer these tests at all to these types of individuals. The legal challenge that arises is if the company was focused on safety, then the organization should screen everyone regularly who is involved in that work area.

Legal Perspective on Drug Testing in the Workplace

When working for the government, there are typically three types of drug testing that could be applied to an individual. The three predominant types of drug testing are pre-employment, accident investigation, and random testing. Pre-employment testing should be conducted consistently across all jobs, or at least for jobs that have potentially safety-related consequences. This type of testing has been consistently upheld and has been found not to be considered an unreasonable search (Beauchamp, 1997). One of the reasons this test has been upheld is that it is conducted before employment, so there is no bond between employer and employee. Without the established employment relationship and only the expectation of employment, this type of testing has been consistently upheld as reasonable (Beauchamp, 1997).

Accident investigation drug testing is another legally acceptable reason to conduct a drug test. When there exists a reasonable question regarding the state of an individual involved in an accident it is considered reasonable for those involved to be subject to a drug test. *Division 241 Amalgamated Transit Union versus Suscy* upheld the rule requiring that a bus driver submits to a drug test after a serious accident (Beauchamp, 1997).

Random testing is mostly considered unreasonable and for the most part illegal. Random testing and surprise mass testing has not been found legal in most states. Random testing has been shown to be an unrealistic method of determining drug use. Although random testing may deter drug use in the workplace, the application of random testing can be particularly difficult to use to separate an employee due to the potential unjust selection of an individual or group for testing.

Existing Company Policy

In light of this information, three anonymous companies will be reviewed with regard to their drug-testing policy. All of these companies strive to offer a safe work environment, and all of these companies have responsibilities for the safety of their guests.

Company A explains that a background check and a pre-employment drug test are required for employment. There is also mention of an annual physical, which will include an annual drug test. Both of these types of drug tests are clear and acceptable by legal standards. Also, in several parts of the pre-employment information, it is mentioned that they take pride in contributing to a safe and drug-free work environment. Durg testing and zero tolerance toward drugs is a common requirement for government positions.

Company B explains that for all new employees there is a background check and a pre-employment drug test. There is also an annual physical, which will include an annual drug test. Company B discloses that the applicant will pay for the initial drug test (between $75 and $220). At first glance, this seems a little much to gain employment, however, by the applicant paying for the drug test there can be no dispute that they are seeking employment and that they were fully aware of the consequences of the drug test. Company B states that it has a zero-tolerance regarding drug testing, and it promotes a safe and drug-free environment. Also, all employees are subject to a zero-tolerance random drug-testing program. The pre-employment information does not explain the "random" process of drug testing, and so the company should have certain safeguards to avoid manipulation or other legal issues.

Company C advises that it may require a pre-employment, rehire, recall, transfer, or re-classification physical examination. This physical examination can include a drug or alcohol test. These physical examinations are also required if a supervisor suspects that an individual is under the influence of drugs or alcohol. It also states that all employees are subject to a physical examination at the discretion of the Company at any time, at the Company's expense. The policy for all employees is that the Company may request that an individual submits to a physical examination at any time or face termination.

Employee Alternatives

Alternatives to individuals who find this type of testing morally unacceptable are limited. The choices are either a careful screening of large corporations or limiting oneself to smaller companies. One can carefully screen available employers to determine if they have an existing drug policy. Individuals seeking alternatives should be aware that companies fully disclose their drug policy or potentially face legal repercussions regarding surprise drug testing that has been found in the past illegal. In 1987, almost 50% of all employers in the Fortune 500 had an existing drug-testing policy (Beauchamp, 1997). Drug policies have been growing steadily since then, and almost all companies now have some drug and alcohol policy.

Summary

In conclusion to this dilemma, there is the final moral question that can only be answered by the individual. The acceptability of drug testing in the workplace becomes a choice of the individual. Although it is not particularly relevant job information for determining productivity, drug testing does deter drug use by employees. When someone holds that individual rights are inviolable, then one would side with privacy rather than potentially helping the good of the company. Of course, drug testing in the workplace may be the first in the long list of personal privacy invasions by unfeeling organizations. However, it appears that for now, society will have to live with the reality of drug testing in the workplace as it is today.

Chapter Twenty—Discussion/Quiz Questions

a. Is ethics important to contracts?

b. Why are ethics and culture important to contracts?

c. Is drug testing in the workplace legal?

d. Why is drug-testing part of the culture of government contracting?

e. Do individuals have rights pertaining to drug testing?

f. Does drug testing create a safe workplace? Why or why not?

g. Does an employer have the right to drug testing during off hours? Why or why not?

h. What impact does the fact that some states have legalized the use of some drugs that are still illegal at the Federal level?

i. Can a drug test be used to decide to hire or not to hire?

j. Can a drug test be required as part of an accident investigation?

k. Do companies have to have a policy regarding drug testing?

l. Can a company charge an employee for a drug test? Why or why not?

m. Can a company charge an individual looking for work at the company for a drug test as part of the application process?

n. This clash of State and Federal Law is not exclusive to drug use. There is a clash between State and Federal laws regarding drones. The FAA (Federal) has issued rules regarding drones; however, the privacy of individuals has always remained the policy area of the State. Will the State or Federal laws prevail?

CHAPTER TWENTY-ONE
ETHICS AND CULTURE IN TRANSPORTATION AND LOGISTICS

Transportation is a complicated business, and there are many laws and regulations that a person might encounter in this business. As with any complex business, there will always be different circumstances and ethical issues that the industry might encounter. In this chapter, several of these ethical and cultural issues will be discussed to show the complex nature of the business of transportation and logistics. The complex issues to be discussed revolve around the use of high-speed rail in the United States, the transportation of products across state lines, the impact of North American Free Trade Agreement (NAFTA), and the rise of economy air carriers.

Although other nations have had success with high-speed rail, high-speed rail has never delivered on the promises that it has made to the American people. Amtrak continues to exist because the government subsidizes the rail service. American railroads have not made money in decades so to move forward with high-speed rail would be another waste of tax payer's money. Also, no high-speed rail program has even been completed on time and budget. It would appear that high-speed rail is just another political move to hand out big contracts to companies that have bought influence in government. Although there are some high-speed rail projects in progress, most of these are coming at the expense of the taxpayer.

Over the history of Amtrak, it has lost $45 billion dollars over its 44 year history (Sabas, 2015). Amtrak cannot even manage to make money on the $9 hamburgers they sell on board because when operating expenses were reviewed it cost Amtrak $16 to produce the hamburger (Sabas, 2015). The U.S. government appears to be willing to pass out subsidies without actually requiring improvements. The U.S. government lacks the will to do the necessary changes to improve passenger railroads. Until the change is required and profitability becomes a priority, there is no reason to invest in passenger rail in the United States. If Amtrak cannot make money on a $9 hamburger, then they should be replaced with an organization that would be willing to take the necessary steps to improve the system.

Although the Uniform Commercial Code (UCC) addresses many of the issues around logistics that cross state lines, the United States has new issues that were not considered by the UCC. Recently, the United States has started to legalize medical and recreational marijuana in different states causing issues when it comes to logistics. The question arises, does the state law takes precedence or does the national law takes precedence.

When there is an intersection between the national and state governments, there can be some issues of jurisdiction. National parks exist in a state, and so there could be an issue of whose laws take precedence in a state park. For example, if a crime were to occur in a national park, under whose jurisdiction is the crime. If someone were to commit a crime in a national park in Colorado, under what jurisdiction is it. Let us assume for the sake of argument; the crime is the possession of marijuana. In the state of Colorado possessing marijuana is not a crime; however, because the person in question brought it into a national park has a law been broken because possessing marijuana is still a national crime. The question becomes what happens to the person in possession of marijuana in the national park in Colorado.

Although there seems to be an issue, in this case, the national law takes priority. So, in this example, a person could be arrested by a friendly ranger in the park for violating the law (PotGuide Colorado, n.d.). The federal law is that a first offender can have up to a year in prison and a $1,000 fine and the fines and jail time increase with multiple convictions (PotGuide Colorado, n.d.). National parks are only under federal laws and enforcement and so even though there will be highways through a national park, state highway patrol would not have any authority on national park grounds. Although the state law allows for possession, if the individual were on federal property, then there would be a crime.

Note that in all cases, the use of marijuana and driving is illegal. There are no laws, state or federal, that allow for an individual to drive while impaired. Also, individuals that drive as an occupation often fall under the Department of Transportation (DOT) rule, which means that not only can a person be criminally prosecuted for operating a vehicle while impaired, but can lose his commercial license for an extended period.

NAFTA has been another interesting change in the logistical landscape of the United States. Despite much hoopla about how NAFTA will improve the United States, it does not appear to have created new jobs for the United States. Although NAFTA supposedly opens the borders between the different nations in North American, there has been more money spent to restrict border crossings than ever before. According to Hazen and Lynch (2008), there still seem to be disputes regarding allowing Mexican truckers into the United States. This situation with truckers from Mexico seems to run counter to the concept of opening up trade borders. It is interesting to note that there does not appear to be any issue to restrict Canadian truck drivers from entering the United States. Even truck drivers from Quebec are not restricted who might only know French. It would appear that there is already a double standard; it clearly shows that NAFTA is not achieving its goals and appears to be only aggravating our neighbors. Perhaps it would be better to eliminate NAFTA and simply go back to agreements that we had individually with Canada and Mexico.

Furthermore, NAFTA seems to be benefiting Canada the most of the three nations. Canada has become the largest trading partner with the United States (Office of the United States Trade Representative: Executive Office of the President, n.d.a). It seems that there has been additional trade due to NAFTA, although the Office of the United States Trade Representative does not make any judgment regarding the impact of NAFTA.

Also, there are only three areas of trade where NAFTA has had an impact on Mexico. There are agreements in place for cement, sweeteners, and tequila (Office of the United States Trade Representative: Executive Office of the President, 2016, Office of the United States Trade Representative: Executive Office of the President, n.d.b). Although these three agreements are important to those involved, it does not appear that these achievements have generated much additional trade. For these reasons, it would appear that NAFTA is another waste of money as it is not working as designed with Mexico and it appears to be benefiting Canada at the expense of the U.S. taxpayer.

Southwest is probably the most well-known and most successful low-cost carrier (LCCs) operating in aviation today. Although several other LCCs operate in the United States and other nations, in recent history the two changes that have happened that have impacted LCCs has been the price of fuel and the airline industry charging for every extra possible. There was a time when traveling on an airplane was an event. One would dress up and expect a meal, some beverages, and everything was included. Flying on a plane was something special.

Fuel costs have dropped significantly recently, yet air tickets have yet to show an equal drop in price. It is estimated that the price of air tickets will drop 1% in 2016, compared to the price of oil being 50% of what is was a couple of years ago (Schlangenstein & Sasso, 2016). Rob Britton of American Airlines defends the lack of the drop in price by comparing it to other industries, like rail or taxis that do not drop their prices when the price of fuel drops (Schlangenstein & Sasso, 2016). It is exactly this kind of thinking that allows the entry of LCCs. If one is not willing to drop the price, other companies will enter the market to make the same kind of profits by offering lower prices. Despite the comments by Rob Britton, the rise of Uber and Lyft shows that taxi companies should be considering a price decrease to stay competitive. Taxi companies do not lower their price, and so the LCCs move in (Uber and Lyft). As for Amtrak, that railway has never made money through its 44 year history so clearly they cannot make a profit with fuel prices being high or low (Sabas, 2015).

Beyond the price of fuel, there are three areas that impact the operating costs of an airline.

1. Reduction of fuel due to more efficient operations

2. Reduction of fuel due to more efficient aircraft operations

3. Reduction of fuel to lower costs rather than worry about on-time operation

For point one, airlines were able to reduce fuel cost be removing un-used equipment like out outlets, logo lights, and old phones (MacLennan, 2013). This cost-savings change was rather innovative because it shows some out of the box thinking. What is even better about this kind of change is that it has no impact on customer satisfaction but resulted in fuel savings for the operation.

For point two, newer aircraft are more fuel efficient but also airplanes waste much fuel on the ground. It is more fuel efficient for an aircraft to get pulled around by ground vehicles. Using ground services more often costs less in fuel (Scott, 2011). I have seen this happen but never really gave it much thought. It is also safer when there is congestion on the ground as the ground vehicle will have better visibility and can navigate better when gates are full.

For point three, which has impacted all of us who have traveled, it is about the weight issue on aircraft. Airlines started charging for baggage and in some cases, it was up to $100 per bag (Davies, 2013). However, now that fuel prices are low, the airlines continue to extract this extra money from consumers. Part of the issue with this is that there is no regulation in this area, and so some airlines charge up to $150 for a bag going in the cargo hold. Let alone if one wants a meal on board, which can cost another $20 or more.

This system of charging for every extra that used to be included is certainly wearing on the consumer. There also have been talks that government might restrict these charges in the future. What is most interesting about this is that Southwest has not moved to the model to charge for luggage. Southwest only had short air routes and so they never offered meals. While other airlines like Spirit charge for food and luggage but often offer the lowest fares, the final costs are typically competitive with Southwest. There is still a place for LCCs however; some simply are more efficient and profitable than others. The strongest issue is that demand for air travel is still high. People are flying more than ever, and that will continue to keep prices high, and it will continue to allow more entrants into the low-cost segment of the airline business.

Summary

In closing, there are some ethical and cultural issues in the transportation industry that impact companies as well as individuals. Individuals must follow and understand the law while in the logistics industry. There are also some laws that appear to benefit some, at the expense of others. Also, companies have a right to make a profit, but there are ethical questions when it would appear that some industries are price gouging. There is always a difficult balance in the transportation industry, not only for companies but for individuals that derive a living from the industry.

Chapter Twenty-One—Discussion/Quiz Questions

a. Is high-speed rail a good idea in the United States?

b. Does high-speed rail save money for the United States?

c. Has Amtrak proven that railroads are still profitable? Why or why not?

d. This clash of State and Federal Law is not exclusive to the transport of marijuana. There is a clash between State and Federal laws regarding drones. The FAA (Federal) has issued rules regarding drones; however, the privacy of individuals has always remained the policy area of the State. Will the State or Federal laws prevail?

e. Has the United States benefited from NAFTA? Why or why not?

f. Does NAFTA allow truckers from Canada and Mexico equal access to drive across national borders?

g. Should the price of airline tickets drop with the drop in the price of oil? Why or why not?

h. Should airlines be regulated to how much they can charge for extras like luggage or food?

i. What are some of the important costs associated with airlines? Are these costs similar to other modes of freight?

CHAPTER TWENTY-TWO
ETHICS AND CULTURE IN REVERSE LOGISTICS

Reverse logistics organizations are virtual organization. Long gone are the days where everyone in the organization was housed in a single location, and because the reverse logistics department will have to work with customer service, production, sales, marketing, returns, repairs, external suppliers, 3PL, not to mention customers and clients, there is no possible way that the reverse logistics organization will be housed in a single building. This concept is important because, in addition to having to manage differently, the head of reverse logistics will need to understand how to leverage the culture of a virtual organization.

An important aspect of a virtual organization is the culture. Project culture can influence personal values by the nature of what is happening in the project. In some cases, a project can be a brand unto itself and so it can resonate with people and cause them to act according to the brand. One might see this in the case where the project is high profile and people feel that it is representative of the company. In this case, the project might be seen as a brand ambassador for other potential clients.

Organizational culture is the culture of the organization. The organization can impart certain views and ideas upon the individual. According to the PMBOK, organizational culture is the norms, shared visions, and shared values of individuals in an organization (Project Management Institute, 2013a). This view can certainly have an impact upon team members and can show up as the organizational work ethics of the people involved as well as the impression regarding acceptable work (Project Management Institute, 2013a).

National culture is the values imparted by the nation that is host to the project. Many times the national culture will dictate policy regarding working hours, holidays, and other work parameters that may influence a project. In many cases because this is such a strong influence, it will certainly direct certain qualities of the project. Project Managers need to be aware of this to leverage culture when and where appropriate in a project. Also, project managers need to lead their organization when it comes to meeting the objectives of reverse logistics.

Leadership in the reverse logistics process is essential for success. For example, a simple return might need to be identified by customer service, then move to production for repair and after repair, it would move to the logistics department, and then finally back to the customer service department. Many reverse logistics scholars believe that a reverse logistics department should be created along with an executive level director or vice president to ensure that the process is done properly (Hoffman, 2006). Other organizations have moved to outsourcing the entire process to achieve better control of the customer process. Regardless of the strategy to address reverse logistics (internal or external), there needs to be a plan and policy that will meet the needs of customers.

The focus on customers and policy is essential. Although different authors had different ideas on how to address customers and policies, all felt that improving the returns process should be a priority and hence should be a best practice for any organization (Blanchard, 2012; Hoffman, 2006). What is interesting about this is that many organizations recognize the importance of customer service, and they recognize that returns are part of customer service, but many still do not want to admit that RLM (or at least returns management) is an important function for the organization. Many times the returns function was combined in the role of another functional manager who would see returns management as a secondary or tertiary role.

Ethics and the Reverse Logistics Body of Knowledge

The Reverse Logistics Body of Knowledge (RLBOK) is to introduce, discuss, and offer application of reverse logistics. There are eight defined domains that explain the various standards for all reverse logistics operations. The RLBOK explains the various areas in the same way that the PMBOK Guide is the standard for project management, or the Contact Management Body of Knowledge (CMBOK) is the standard for contract managers. The RLBOK will explain the various areas of reverse logistics applications and theory. In turn, this will define the field of reverse logistics by offering definitions regarding ethics, knowledge, strategies, and technologies that can impact the success of the commercial, government, military, and non-profit organizations in carrying out reverse logistics operations.

Summaries of the Eight Domains of Reverse Logistics

Domain 1—Market Research

The emergence of the importance of reverse logistics has been a market-driven process. Because reverse logistics continues to increase in importance within organizations, a structured practice of market research and data analysis is required. Reverse logistics recognizes that it is a dynamic area of research and because of this, reverse logistics must continuously evolve and grow dynamically through continuous improvement. Reverse logistics realizes that market forces are changing and the only way to remain an essential organizational function and the operational area is to embrace the market. Reverse logistics embraces new technology and systems and management practices to meet the growing needs of the market, while preserving privacy and leaving the control of data to the individual(s) that own the information.

Domain 2—Strategic Planning

A strategic plan for reverse logistics operations provides direction and guidance for how coordinated activities can result in success. Dynamic reverse logistics includes both short-term and long-term objectives based on internal and competitive analysis and organizational preferences. Understanding critical business issues and success factors allows an organization to develop tactical initiatives and decision models that can be used on an on-going basis to achieve the objectives outlined in the strategic plan. The strategic plan must abide by the ethical and legal requirements as set forth by the nation, the company, and the field.

Domain 3—Innovation

All logistical matters pertain to process and innovation. Successful logistical organizations cannot maintain long-term success without a process improvement cycle that supports innovation. Reverse logistics strives to create a process framework that supports long-term success and innovation. Reverse logistics processes should leverage process improvement. Innovation cannot sacrifice the ethics of the organization or the external perception of the firm. Whenever possible, innovation should also support sustainability.

Domain 4—Project and Process

A common framework should connect reverse logistics projects. Returns, recycling, recalls, and repackaging become project-based activities. Reverse logistics seeks to offer a common project platform that supports solutions to issues regarding returns recycling, recalls, and repackaging. A common project framework allows for a successful organization to address each project-based activity leading efficiently and ultimately to success. These areas of reverse logistics are projects and must adhere to the ethical requirements of not only the nation, the organization, but also to the code of ethics associated with project management.

Domain 5—Cost and Benefits

Reverse logistics is not just about customer service; it is about building a successful organization. A cost-benefit process not only finds the direct costs but quantifies the indirect costs and savings. An organization cannot ignore direct costs and savings, but one should not forget the indirect losses that can occur when customers have a negative experience. One cannot directly quantify the lifetime losses of a single customer, but one can certainly understand the failure of customers to return to an organization. One single improper return or recall can lose a customer for life. Understanding that short-term gains can lead to long-term losses creates an organizational ethical conundrum that needs to be addressed by reverse logistics.

Domain 6—Communication

A reverse logistics organization exists to serve customers, and so a reverse logistics organization must align the majority of its communications outward. Internal communication is essential, but internal communication should mirror external communication. An effective reverse logistics organization should manage information at both the macro- and the micro-levels. Microdata consist of the information associated with the communication directly to the customer. Macrodata consist of the information associated with the communication that comes indirectly to the customer, such as the media. The organization needs to behave ethically and responsibly so that both the microdata and macrodata are congruent and consistent.

Domain 7—Leadership

Effective leadership drives successful RLM, and an organization cannot harness the potential of the human resources available without effective leadership. RLM has chosen to focus on transformational leadership because transformational leadership has been shown to be effective during times of change. Transformational leadership can not only assist in a successful reverse logistics organization, but these skills can also improve the organization. As with any leadership style, the leader must be bound to be loyal to the organization, the nation, and the stakeholders. Leaders who behave ethically and morally are those whom people will want to follow in the short and long terms.

Domain 8—Research Data

Reverse logistics seeks to utilize research data protecting measures to not only protect the customer but to protect all parties involved, directly or indirectly, in the process. These measures not only cover the ethical concerns surrounding data, but it also includes the safekeeping and security involved. Data protecting measures must remain as an essential aspect of reverse logistics so that customers and potential customers feel secure in the processes. Reverse logistics processes might involve the sensitive data of customers; there exists a need for the respect for privacy as well as for the safekeeping of research data.

Summary

The RLBOK is clearly a WIP. Although it has outlined the field and it offers insights into successful ethics and culture, there is still work to be done. Ultimately, there will be more individuals skilled and educated in reverse logistics, and they will be helping to retrain organizations toward greater efficiency. Human resources will certainly be at the core of these changes. However, there are some technologies that will also help the field grow and evolve.

Chapter Twenty-Two—Discussion/Quiz Questions

a. What is a virtual organization?

b. Does reverse logistics use virtual organizations?

c. Is culture an important part of virtual organizations? Why or why not?

d. Does national culture impact a project?

e. Why is leadership important in reverse logistics?

f. What is the Reverse Logistics Body of Knowledge?

g. What is Domain 1 of the Reverse Logistics Body of Knowledge?

h. What is Domain 2 of the Reverse Logistics Body of Knowledge?

i. What is Domain 3 of the Reverse Logistics Body of Knowledge?

j. What is Domain 4 of the Reverse Logistics Body of Knowledge?

k. What is Domain 5 of the Reverse Logistics Body of Knowledge?

l. What is Domain 6 of the Reverse Logistics Body of Knowledge?

m. What is Domain 7 of the Reverse Logistics Body of Knowledge?

n. What is Domain 8 of the Reverse Logistics Body of Knowledge?

CHAPTER TWENTY-THREE
SUMMARY

Effective leadership is essential in contract management, transportation and logistics, and RLM. An organization cannot harness the true potential of the human resources available without effective leadership. Given that leadership research has shown that transformational leadership is effective during times of change, contract management, transportation and logistics, and RLM focus on transformational leadership as a best practice.

Organizational leadership is the process of piecing together the puzzle of information in order to get the big picture. The mark of a good leader of an organization is the one that can assimilate all of these data and create a view that is consistent and accurate of the organization. Leaders bring together great groups that have individual and specific purposes, without losing the elements of creativity and independence. Although one can fault the organization for not providing a road map, this will often not change the situation.

To conceptualize this better, view an organization like an onion. Each of the sections of an onion is so tightly pressed together that it appears to be a solid ball, yet the reality is that each "leaf" is only connected at the base. Each layer is not directly connected, and yet they are all connected to the base. Moreover, from all outward appearances the onion is a single vegetable.

Think of operations leadership as an onion. Management and leadership is all about seeing the difference of human constructs and being able to move that organization from homeostasis toward a particular goal. People want to retain their individuality without losing their identity. They want to be part of a greater whole, yet they want to remain independent of the rest. This is the great paradox of social systems.

Flexible systems are those that can react to new situations. Organizations that are tightly integrated without being co-dependent are the direction that the organizations of the future will take. In the past, organizations strove to be a homogenous mass, completely intertwined, with no room for sudden change. Now, organizations must become more resilient and flexible without losing sight of the whole or the individual.

Although there are some ethical and cultural challenges in the area of developing an integrated supply chain the need for good leadership cannot be ignored. Maintaining industry and organizational values is essential to transformational leadership. Once the values are understood by all and then modeled by the transformational leader, the values will operate as the core beliefs of the group to guide them through the changes that lie ahead.

Reverse logistics needs transformational leaders that are versed in the scope and deliverables of a reverse logistics department and also must be versed in the needs of the customer. Also, the leader must understand the goals and objectives of the reverse logistics organization. To this end, the transformational leader must understand some of the hidden dynamics of organizational decision-making processes to achieve the goals of the organization. Organizational dynamics are human systems and are rarely simplistic, so a good transformational leader must be able to adapt and apply these toward the goal of the reverse logistics function and that of the organization.

Contract management and logistics management require a transformational leader who can change direction as needed and can create a *new* plan to achieve the same goal. The functional areas must be willing to reinvent themselves, their department, and their organizational objectives to meet the needs of the customer and the company. Furthermore, because supply chain is a growing field, the leader of the supply chain within an organization should have a long-term plan to keep everyone on track, and he or she should align this plan with the ultimate goals of the company. The goal of the contract, logistics, and reverse logistics managers is to keep everyone moving toward the common goal. Also, the leader must have the capacity to get people back on track if they stray from the plan.

In closing, a transformational leader must be able to adapt to a world of rapid change, while remaining true to core values. A transformational leader understands that the plan may change, but the organizational values and the needs of the customer must remain at the forefront of the plan. Leaders who remain true to their core values will be able to offer a banner of stability that will help others cope with the change which all organizations must undergo. Thus, a transformational leader is the one who can operate with a flag of immutable core values while navigating a sea of change.

Chapter Twenty-Three—Discussion/Quiz Questions

a. Is effective leadership important?

b. What is transformational leadership?

c. Are goals and objectives important to leadership?

d. Should leaders be able to punish those that stray off course?

e. How is organizational leadership like an onion?

f. Does a leader need to be ethical?

g. Is transformational leadership important in contracts? Why or why not?

SECTION SIX
FUTURE PERSPECTIVES

CHAPTER TWENTY-FOUR
THE FUTURE OF MODERN PROJECT, PROGRAM, AND PORTFOLIO MANAGEMENT

Communication should be a fundamental strength in any project, program, or portfolio; however, more organizations are feeling pressure to achieve greater efficiency. When the pressure becomes too demanding, communications is one of the first things to be set aside. What organizations do not realize is that social skills are probably more important as cost, scope, and schedule. If people are not being managed correctly, confusion will ensue. Hence, it is essential to maintain good communication throughout the life of the project, program, or portfolio.

Experienced project managers will try to use the same team for almost every project. The reason is that project managers have already invested time and energy into those relationships. It not only takes time to build up new relationships, it often will take additional time. With slim budgets and short time frames, a project manager will seek to avoid building new relationships when a prior relationship might suffice.

In some cases, the project manager feels that they are more responsible for communication than the deliverables for a project. A demanding client will ask for updates and information regularly, making additional management and oversight of others difficult.

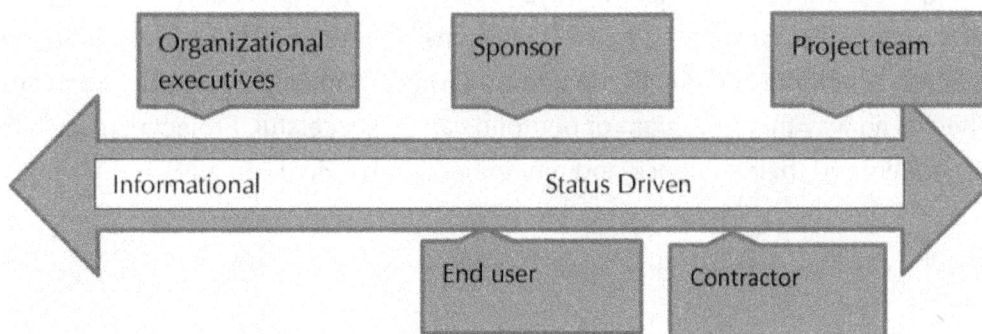

Figure 9: Information flows and stakeholders

Although the project manager might be tempted to use a one size fits all communication strategy, communication needs to be different for different individuals involved with the project (Figure 9). The communication to the sponsor and the end user should be a good balance of project information and status information. The sponsor and end user require up to date information about the project. The communication to the end user should be a little more informational as the sponsor will be more milestones driven than will be the end user.

Communication with the project team should be very status driven as all the aspects of the project team will revolve around deadlines. The communication should be more exact and less informational as project team members need to know the details. In this regard, the communication with a contractor should be similar to project team communication as the contractor is involved with a project. The contractor will also be very task oriented and needs to be aware of looming deadlines and other dependencies.

Organizational executives need communication that is at a very high informational level. Organizational executives are less interested in status as they just want to know if the project is on time and budget or not. If it is not on time or budget, they need to know the plan to bring it back on schedule or to bring the costs back in line. Therefore, information with this group needs to be concise and clear without many details. Share the milestones and the completed aspects of the project and share high-level details on what is being done to keep or get a project back on track.

Summary

In closing, there are several different ways to manage communication within a project, program, or portfolio. However, a lot of the responsibility rests with the individual project manager. Without input and details regarding a project from the responsible project manager, there is no way that a program or portfolio can be successful. Project managers must learn to understand their audience and remember that brevity is an ally.

Chapter Twenty-Four—Discussion/Quiz Questions

a. Is communication important for modern Project, Program and Portfolio Management?

b. Why do people want to work in the same teams?

c. Identify information flows and stakeholders

d. Should all stakeholders receive the same type and level of communication?

e. Are some stakeholders more important than others?

f. Should the sponsor and an end user get the same type and level of communication?

g. Does the project team need up to date information about the project?

h. Does understanding the audience matter when it comes to communication?

CHAPTER TWENTY-FIVE
THE FUTURE OF CONTRACTING AND ACQUISITION

According to the CMBOK, the three core competencies are technical, conceptual, and human relations (NCMA, 2013). All three of these will certainly evolve and change in the future. However, not all of them will change at the same rate. There already is a shift in certain technical definitions in contracts, given the basis of these as part of the legal system these are likely to be the slowest to change. Conceptual is already being shaped as there are new concepts of liability and responsibility as self-guided technology is evolving. Finally, human relations will likely move quickly given the changes in transportation technology.

As previously stated, the legal systems will unlikely change rapidly in the future. Contacts are clearly defined and have been defined for some time. Although there is the potential that certain codes will change in the future, such as the UCC, this is not likely to happen with any alacrity.

Conceptual skills for contract managers will have to change quickly to maintain a grasp upon changing technology and changing ideas. The leap from self-piloting vehicles, the use of unmanned aerial vehicles (UAV) and robots and the associated technologies will certainly disrupt contracts. These new constructs will change liability in ways never seen before. Government agencies are already falling behind with regulations as the FAA has struggled to publish new rules regarding UAV technology, even after people are already being prosecuted for using them in prohibited areas. Government contracting agencies will need to understand these technologies in a broader sense that will impact the language and direction that these contracts take.

Human relations skills are always very important, but the level of technology that is currently available could mean that there will be less human contact in the future. Self-piloting trucks, self-piloting forklifts, robots, and drones in warehouses almost sounds impossible today, but all of these technologies are getting close to fruition. Conventional wisdom states that people will always want to interact with other people, and so a personal touch will always be part of contracts. However, the children of today are growing up with technology at their fingertips. Computer friends and robotic tutors are educating our children. The question that arises is that will the next generation prefer these robotic playmates to people?

Summary

In closing, the future of contracts and procurement is not yet written. There are still many twists and turns that the industry and society can take. Although technology will drive logistics and reverse logistics, the automation of contracts and contractual relationships is not quite here. However, given the rate of change in the other areas, it is only a matter of time.

Chapter Twenty-Five—Discussion/Quiz Questions

a. Will contract management change in the future? Why or why not?

b. Why will the legal system not change rapidly in the future?

c. Does the concept of a contract need revision? Why or why not?

d. Will UAV change contracts in the future?

e. Will there be more government oversight of contracts in the future?

f. Will new technologies like self-piloting cars change the nature of human relations in contracts?

g. Are human relation skills becoming more or less important?

h. Will robots replace humans in certain jobs in the future? Why or why not?

CHAPTER TWENTY-SIX
THE FUTURE OF TRANSPORTATION AND LOGISTICS

Intermodal Freight of the Future

Although sea freight and rail are currently the most popular form of intermodal freight, there is a growing consensus that this will change in the coming decades. There is no doubt that sea and rail will still be an important part of any organization's supply chain, logistics is on the cusp of a new generation of intermodal freight. Looking forward, one has to recognize the growing importance of autonomous delivery systems (ADS). Drones, terrestrial robots, or self-piloting rail vehicles will soon dominate the "last mile" of delivery.

Some might feel that this might be a little premature, but people have forgotten that these devices already operate among us, and no one is taking notice. Amazon has begun an aggressive acquisition program to create a global network of logistics as well as they have also become a manufacturer of delivery drones (Amazon, n.d.). Although some feel that this is premature, both Germany and Switzerland are already using drones to deliver mail. This new technology has the potential to disrupt the old system of movement of goods. Large delivery style drones have recently been approved by the FAA, but no company has started using them for last mile retail applications. However, a company is China is already making retail deliveries by drone (Araujo, 2016).

The UK is already testing terrestrial autonomous robots to deliver groceries locally in London (Tablyn, 2016). The Botler (an automated hotel robot) has already been in use at hotels for almost a year (Gaudin, 2015). These technologies seem more likely to be accepted due to not violating our airspace, but greater acceptance will certainly come in time. Furthermore, a mining company in Australia is already using self-piloting trucks to make regular deliveries in a remote area (Clark, 2015).

Another consideration that has crept up and no one has cried foul is self-piloting rail vehicles. Self-piloting trains are common in many airports, and these robotic railcars carry hundreds of thousands of people, if not millions of people daily with rarely an incident. There is already a company working to create a small robot train delivery system that could be integrated as part of a city (Nield, 2015). There is no doubt that more of this kind of technology will be used in the future as additional logistical support is required to support the growing demand of consumers.

 In closing, intermodal freight will certainly be changing over the next several years. It is not surprising that robots and drones will be reinventing society as there has been a shift in intermodal freight that occurs every few decades or so. Clearly, ADS offers disruptive technology that will change the appearance of intermodal freight for the remainder of the century.

The Loss of the Concept of Distance

The concept of distance is already eroding in the global marketplace. People consider how soon they can get something, not how far away it is. The cost of freight is impacted by distance. Many freight companies consider distance and speed when it comes to establishing the cost of delivery. However, the concept of distance is becoming muddled, and this will impact freight, passengers, and information but not in the same linear manner. Due to physical limitations, it is cheaper to send something local than it is to send something to another country. Also, it is easier and cheaper to make an overnight delivery in the same state, than to accomplish the same for a delivery going from Florida to California. Distance will certainly impact freight because it will require more resources to move something further and faster than it does to move something closer and slower. Moving things across the country can be achieved by truck, rail, sea, or air; however, if it needs to get there quickly, it will likely have to move by air (and truck for the last mile).

Passengers, like freight, can go by car, rail, sea, or air as well. Again we see the connection between distance and time when it comes to passengers. Passengers that are willing to take more time to travel can consider car, rail, and sea, as those options tend to take longer. However, with passenger travel, every mode of slower travel does not equate to lower costs. For example, trains are considerably slower than air travel but trains are not much cheaper than air travel. Of course, there are specials and other kinds of discount rates, but rail travel has not been a great economic deal for passengers. One can find a more competitive rate by bus or air. The passenger transportation becomes a function of supply and demand. However, rail seems to have less pressure to become more efficient and offers better rates due to government subsidies. Amtrak seems to lose money every year and Congress finds money to bail them out. Airline struggles or another airline buys them to get to their assets and routes. It is strange that every country in Europe can run a profitable rail system, but somehow that is not possible in the United States.

Information is the most interesting with regard to distance. Information defies the laws of supply and demand. Information does not have to be limited by the cost–distance relationship of freight and passengers. In fact, information is governed by its laws and rules. One can ship a book from the United States to Estonia, and the book would have to travel by some freight carrier and clear international customs when it arrives at Estonia. The book would be subject to the same limitations as freight. If a person were to carry that book on a flight to Estonia, when the person arrived, the book would be considered personal belongings and would come along as luggage when one arrives in the country. A person would clear customs, but likely a customs official would not care that a passenger brought a book along for a long flight.

However, because the information of the book does not need to be transported physically, the information of the book can transcend the limitations and requirements of freight and passengers. Instead, a person could arrive in Estonia by air and go to Amazon while in the hotel and download the book without any concern regarding distance and freight. The information would be delivered without having to pass through international customs. The download would have little relationship with supply and demand of the cost of the physical book. Thus, there are a lot of different elements that impact the supply and demand relationship. Freight and passengers are similar in many regard. However, information seems to be something altogether different in today's digital society.

Chapter Twenty-Six—Discussion/Quiz Questions

a. Will intermodal freight change in the future?

b. Will drones change freight in the future? Why or why not?

c. Will all countries accept drones?

d. Will robots be preferred for delivery over drones in the future?

e. Are robots going to eliminate jobs in logistics in the future?

f. Explain the concept of distance.

g. What is changing about our current concept of distance?

h. What is more important, time or distance, with regard to freight?

i. Can information pass national boarders without inspection?

CHAPTER TWENTY-SEVEN
THE FUTURE OF REVERSE LOGISTICS

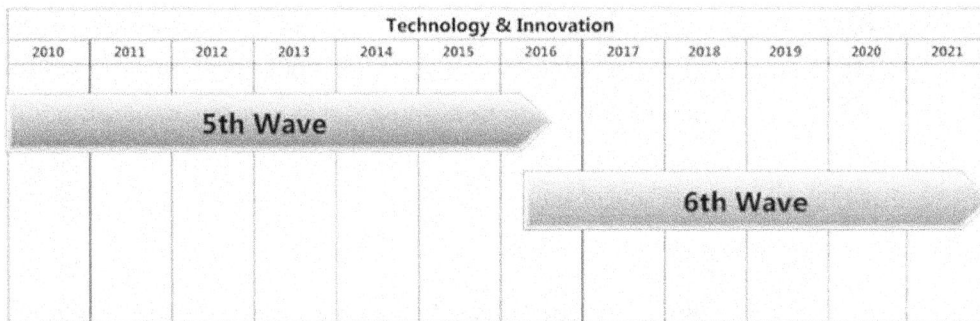

Figure 10: Waves of technology

The Sixth Wave

The future of reverse logistics rests upon the 6th wave of technology (Figure 10). As society emerges from the 5th wave which was about the expansion of handheld devices and the ubiquitous Smartphone, there is more of a focus on the environment and the conservation of resources. Handheld devices are already superseding the use of personal computers. The 6th wave is all about the reduction of waste and doing more with less (Nogrady, 2010). There are clearly more environmentally sound technologies being developed to address the increasing shortage of rare materials on the planet. Although some feel that the planet has an infinite wealth of resources, the reality is that the resources on the planet are quite finite and are being used up faster than ever before.

According to Popular Science, Tesla managed 200,000 preorders for the Model 3 in 24 hours (Franzen, 2016). Tesla has 7.5 billion dollars in sales on a product that has not been fully developed yet. There are already 7.5 billion reasons that we are already moving toward a 6th technology innovation wave where people want more done with renewable resources. The population of the planet is becoming more cognizant of the challenges regarding resources, and they want to make a difference. Being environmental is no longer a fad, it is rapidly becoming a business imperative. Organizations are moving toward zero waste. In fact, in some nations, waste has become illegal. France has recently passed a law requiring that grocery stores are not allowed to throw away food (waste). Grocery stores are required to donate food to eliminate waste (Frej, 2016). Society has clearly changed, and although the time frame presented for the 5th wave is listed at 1990–2020, it is clear that the 6th wave is already upon us.

The future means change and change means making a start. The usual problem with organizations is that there is no owner to address these small issues. Instead, they remain as small problems that never seem to reach the top of the list of important matters for the day. In some cases, the recommendations are not only good for an organization but they are also good for the individual. In this case, it is often a good idea to do these changes in one's life to make the changes at work. If one can embody these changes, they are more likely to get others to change as well.

According to Stringer (2009), there are three easy changes that can make a big difference in wasted resources. First, one should replace all incandescent lights with compact fluorescent or LED lights (Stringer, 2009, p. 144). Second, make a conscious effort to turn off all unnecessary lights or use dimmers or motion sensors to turn off lights while not in use to conserve energy (Stringer, 2009, p. 144). Third, use energy star equipment or utilize equipment that shuts off when not in use (Stringer, 2009, p. 145). These are three easy changes that do not require huge investments but will reduce wasted energy. Once an organization sees the focus upon not wasting energy, then other new ideas will emerge that could save the company even more money in the future.

Future of Technology in Reverse Logistics

Given the rate of change in technology, there is no question that our lives are going to change. Changes in technology will certainly change the everyday lives of people. In particular, there are two technologies that will significantly influence the future of reverse logistics. First, is the widespread use of self-driving vehicles. Second is how the automation of returns will change our perception of the returns process.

First, for logistics, the use of self-driving trucks is going to revolutionize the transportation of materials from distribution center to retail outlet and ultimately to the consumer. Walmart is already developing a truck of the future. The Walmart WAVE truck offers self-driving capabilities along with other improvements that will improve safety and change how material moves from place to place (Walmart, 2014). If one were to take the efficiencies gained by the Walmart WAVE system and combine it with the self-driving capabilities of the Mercedes-designed Future Truck, one could have an amazing new truck that would change shipping. This new technology would represent a significant leap forward in not only self-piloting technology but it would also represent significant improvements in safety as well as creating systems that combat driver fatigue, which is often a factor in accidents involving commercial vehicles (Davies, 2014). Self-driving cars are not as far off as we might think as projections are estimating the self-driving car market will be at 87 billion dollars by 2030 (Rauwald & Tschampa, 2014).

Although self-driving vehicles does not mean that there will be no one at the wheel, it does offer the potential of fewer accidents. It might mean fewer drives are there in some nations that are not requiring a human driver to be onboard. From a safety standpoint, self-driving vehicles never get distracted, they never feel fatigue, and never drive at anything <100%. Driver distraction is an issue as many accidents involving trucks have pointed to fatigue being a factor. This technology will certainly evolve over time and acceptance might be slow at first, but in time it will become a requirement. When seatbelts were first introduced as a safety device, the public was tepid at their introduction. There was a similar situation with the introduction of the first airbags. Over time, as the safety and value of these items were found, they became a requirement for all vehicles. Self-driving vehicles will likely follow the same pattern of acceptance.

Second, for reverse logistics, there will soon be a technology revolution concerning the processing of returns. Most people have used a self-checkout system; however, this same technology could be applied to returns. Using the same technology for self-service checkout is going to revolutionize returns. Imagine instead of standing in the return line, one can go to a station designed to check a return seamlessly and generate a gift card for store credit.

The system would be the same as combining the customer service robot along with a self-checkout station. The self-checkout station would weigh the item being returned, as well as being able to scan the bar code and the bar code on the receipt. If everything comes up as correct, the checkout station could dispense a gift card with the correctly credited value. Just like with self-checkout stations, this would allow a single employee to monitor several returns stations, effectively reducing costs and increasing efficiency.

Both of these changes are going to change how large retailers are going to conduct their logistics and reverse logistics. In both these cases, the technology is still not perfected; however, these changes are going to happen sooner than people think. Technology is moving faster as everyone is trying to apply technological solutions to everyday situations.

Chapter Twenty-Seven—Discussion/Quiz Questions

a. What is the 6th wave of technology?

b. Why is reverse logistics important in the 6th wave of technology?

c. Do people want to live in a greener manner in the future? Why or why not?

d. Should grocery stores in the United States be forced to donate food rather than waste it?

e. Should people use more efficient lighting? Why or why not?

f. Are people trying to conserve more energy than in the past? Why or why not?

g. Will technology change in the future for reverse logistics?

h. Will self-driving trucks become more common in the future?

i. Do you trust self-driving technology? Why or why not?

j. Do you feel that distracted drivers are causing more accidents on the road today?

k. Is an automated return system realistic? Why or why not?

CHAPTER TWENTY-EIGHT
CONCLUSION

Transportation technology has reached a tipping point where it is driving economic growth in several nations. The United States has been driving technological innovation in this area for some time as U.S. companies move toward the additional use of robotics, self-piloting vehicles as well as the increased use of unmanned autonomous vehicles (UAVs). These technologies are going to change contracts, and forward and reverse logistics. Clearly, these three types of transportation technology and innovation will stimulate economic growth for many years to come.

Robotics has started to change the nature of transportation. Although manufacturing uses robots extensively, the most interesting use of robots comes in the form of pizza delivery (Volpicelli, 2016). Domino's uses robots to deliver pizza in New Zealand. This application has certainly changed our perception of the usefulness of robots and how they will start to change our perceptions about logistics. Although robot delivery appears to be a great marketing coup for Dominos, it is clear that the pizza wars continue to move toward robotics as a long-term solution. Pizza Hut announced that they will be deploying robot order takers into locations in the Far East (Curtis, 2016). It seems that the logistics of pizza has to take a huge step forward.

Robotics also seems to be the way that companies will address economic growth. Many in the fast food industry feel that the pending new minimum wage of $15 will accelerate robotics in the United States. This shift to robotics might mean fewer menial jobs, but it could then justify fewer employees who make $15 an hour. Robotics will be changing the landscape of logistics and moving the U.S. economy forward. There is no doubt that the perfection of these technologies will occur in less litigious societies. Once the robotic technology becomes common in other countries, then these companies will move the technology to the United States. A delivery robot (drone) is already being tested in London, so if this testing is successful, there is no doubt that other major cities will follow their lead (Tablyn, 2016).

Self-piloting vehicles continue to grab headlines in logistics as more companies work to perfect the technology. It appears that not only are the major car manufacturers racing to perfect the technology, but even companies like Google, Lyft, and Uber are all testing this technology. Some manufacturers are already announcing that this technology will be available in cars in a few years, and the current Tesla vehicle has some limited self-piloting ability. Although many people are not ready to accept this kind of technology, there are many organizations pouring much money to get it to work. Elon Musk has billions of dollars in orders for his Model 3 vehicles that will include self-piloting technology (Franzen, 2016). The question that emerges from this is what will happen to human truck drivers once the self-piloting technology becomes accepted.

Despite issues in the United States, there is already a fleet of self-piloting trucks operating in Australia (Clark, 2015). This fleet is in operation hauling ore from a mining area to an ore processing area. This successful application of replacing truck drivers is a foreshadowing of the future of ground logistics. Although this has not been approved yet in the United States, there is a mounting success in other nations that means there will be automation in this sector shortly. Also, this change in transportation will change the cost structure for trucking. Self-piloting trucks will lead to other forms of transportation to adapt in a similar fashion to remain competitive. Without labor costs and equipment that can operate around the clock, there will be a fundamental shift in the overall costs of transportation. This reduction in costs will drive economic development worldwide.

UAVs are already changing the last mile of logistics. Despite issues with the FAA in the United States regarding the regulation of UAVs, there are other nations already moving forward with retail deliveries by UAVs, notably China. Amazon is testing this technology in other nations as a means of last mile delivery (Associated Press, 2014). Amazon is not just looking for great marketing; one should consider that the U.S. Postal service has already shortlisted an octocopter as a new delivery vehicle for mail (Mathews, 2015).

It is clear that someone is going to find a way to make this technology economically successful, and then the proliferation will begin. Once an organization can find a cost-effective way to leverage this technology, then there will be a steady competition to make the technology better, cheaper, and faster. It is unclear if it will be Amazon or another company that will harness this new form of logistics, but what is clear is that it will certainly drive economic growth.

There are significant advances and changes in logistics that will change the field in the next 3–7 years. The more those companies will invest in these technologies, the faster that business will use them. Once people use these technologies throughout the world, the sooner robots, self-piloting vehicles, and UAVs will stimulate national economic growth. Elon Musk has billions in preorders, which is certainly amounting to many new jobs. Self-piloting trucks will certainly stimulate demand for new technology. In fact, Nvidia, a gaming company, is moving from video games to technology for self-driving vehicles (LaMonica, 2016). For drones alone, there are an estimated 100,000 new jobs to emerge due to UAV technology (Fernholz, 2013). It is clear that these innovative technologies in logistics will lead to some economic growth.

In conclusion, these innovative technologies continue to revolutionize contracts, forward and reverse logistics, and will change how people perceive the transportation industry as a whole. These sweeping changes in technology will change the global expectation of goods. No longer will overnight be fast enough; these innovative technologies will move society to a point where immediate delivery is a business reality. Innovators should watch these technologies take advantage of these successes and hopefully logistics innovators of the future will build upon these early successes to create future successes.

Chapter Twenty-Eight—Discussion/Quiz Questions

a. Do you feel that robots will stimulate economic growth in the United States?

b. Will autonomous drones become common in the future?

c. Should there be a concern about these kinds of technologies?

d. Is the potential for technology jobs realistic? Why or why not?

e. Is pizza delivery by drone something that will happen in the future? Why or why not?

f. Is society reaching a point where overnight is going to be too long a wait?

SECTION SEVEN
CONTRACTS WORKBOOK

CASE STUDY: RIVER CRUISE COMPANY

All organizations can benefit from improving their supply chain strategy, and a River Cruise Company is no different. The supply chain challenges for any ship are complex; however, for river ships where storage is almost non-existent, a good supply chain strategy is necessary to make sure all the necessary supplies are on board to meet the needs of the guests. However, implementing a successful contract that can address the logistics involved with a river cruise company can be challenging due to short delivery windows, loading restrictions as well as other geographical and national rules or laws. The contract will need to consider the existing supply chain, the business metrics to track, and the recommended supply chain initiatives and innovation.

Existing Supply Chain

The existing organizational supply chain consists of the processes of assessing, forecasting, and fulfilling the procurement needs of the organization (Blanchard, 2010). The essence of supply chain management is the development of a strategic approach toward the supply of goods and services that support an operation. The successful acquisition of goods and services when needed and according to a developed plan creates a successful operation which supports the guests and crew of the river vessel (Hazen & Lynch, 2008). Effective supply chain planning enables the identification of pricing and service opportunities that capture savings. Savings are derived from the efficient operation, reduced transportation costs, and economies of scale.

Also, the organization understands that an investment in training can not only improve the operation but can reduce transactional costs. Part of this will include the operational analysis of not only the plan but all ancillary and secondary costs of procurement. To this end, one must examine the transactional costs, landed costs, as well as the supporting costs to understand the full costs of materials and services for vessel operations.

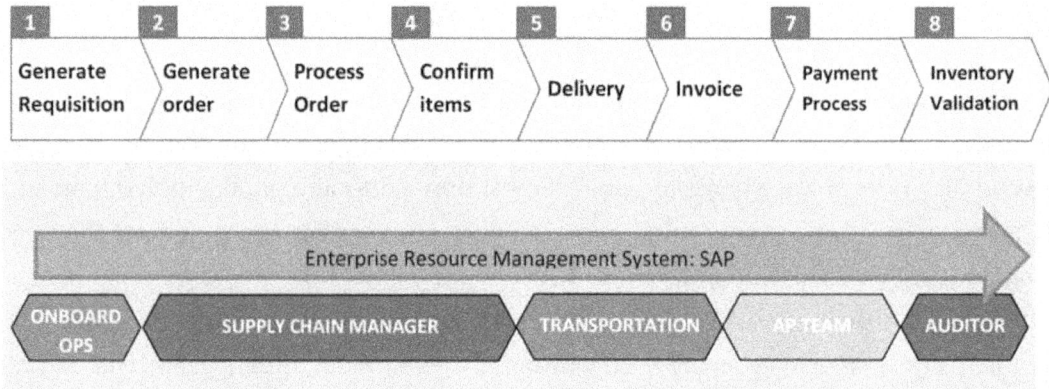

Figure 11: Existing supply chain operation

Figure 11 visually describes the existing supply chain operations to explain the various steps in the process. This process shows the existing enterprise resource planning (ERP) integration as well as the supply, transportation, and payment mechanisms for the organization.

Business Metrics

The current organizational target is for suppliers and transportation companies to be offering a level of 95% accuracy. Currently, suppliers need to maintain a fill rate of 95% or higher in the following categories: Adherence to agreed price by contract and on the invoice, adherence to agreed specifications as outlined by the company, adherence to agreed quantities on order, and adherence to agreed delivery cost, time, and date. Although this target has been met by the majority of the suppliers and transportation companies have adhered to this standard, it is not always enforced. However, moving forward, the organization is growing to a point where this level is no longer meeting the needs of the organization.

Moving forward there needs to be a shift to move to the most accurate suppliers (supplier reduction) to achieve the 99% accuracy that the organization needs to support the current rate of growth. Additional tracking for accuracy is necessary to initiate steps to eliminate or reduce the suppliers that do not meet the 99% accuracy rate. Keep in mind that every mistake in transportation and freight will cost the company more money to recover from the mistake (Boyer & Verma, 2010).

Supply Chain Initiatives

Currently, the organization is looking to move forward with three initiatives that will move the organization forward. These initiatives are moving toward radio frequency identification (RFID), additional supply chain training for the organization and suppliers and the implementation of various incentives for transportation and suppliers. These initiatives should help move the organization forward as well as to apply additional innovation which is ahead of the competition.

The organization currently uses the enterprise resource planning system SAP throughout the enterprise, and so it would be beneficial to leverage the existing RFID interface to improve operations. Using RFID can limit waste, limit the loss of materials, and reduce expensive rush orders (Hedgepeth, Henrie, & Hedgepeth Jr., n.d.). The shift to using RFID can assist in improving the accuracy of transportation and delivery as well as to reduce time in checking, inventorying, and auditing. It is understood that this will require a project team and project timeline to be developed to make this change, however, it can ultimately reduce costs, increase efficiency, and reduce transportation delays. RFID information can flow through the entire system through SAP allowing all aspects of the organization to share the same up to date information as well as to be able to track material in transit effectively.

Because the organization is growing considerably in the short term, there is a great need for additional training in SAP for the growing number of individuals involved with the system. Furthermore, additional resources need to be applied to start using the data held in the system. Different departments need to have at least one SAP superuser to leverage the information gathered by the system. Empowering and training the organization to leverage the information will lead to innovation (Wisner et al., 2012). Without an investment in SAP training, the organization will not utilize the available information and will not be gathering the necessary business intelligence to run more efficiently and reduce costs. For example, supply chain users should be analyzing all data points with regard to transportation companies to determine which ones are most effective and efficient in what regions.

An incentive for transportation companies is one method to help make an organization interested in moving toward the 99% accuracy level. There is no doubt that a transportation organization will incur additional costs from moving from 95% to 99% accuracy. Additional checks and accuracy inspections are necessary to assure the accuracy of delivery. For example, a delivery accuracy of 95% could be achieved by having a single check system where only one person reviews the order before it being shipped. However, one company that was guaranteeing 99% delivery accuracy used a triple check system where three separate people would inspect a delivery for accuracy before it leaves their dock. This triple check system no doubt cost the company time and money to have three separate people inspect an order. Triple check inspection systems will incur additional costs. Offering a financial benefit would address these additional costs that a transportation company might incur. Additionally, this incentive could help transportation suppliers to focus more on our company because our organization would offer greater profit potential (Figure 12).

Initiative	Low cost	High cost	Implementation (months)	ROI period (months)
RFID	$50,000	$100,000	6	18
SAP training	$20,000	$40,000	3	24
Incentive	$15,000	$15,000	3	10

Figure 12: Initiative projected costs

Case Study Questions

1. Given these alternatives, rank these initiatives(s) to make a recommended to the River Cruise Company to budget for the next fiscal year?

2. What is the best alternative from a financial standpoint if the River Cruise Company needed to select the best overall option that would offer the company the greatest impact?

CASE STUDY: PROPOSAL SUPPORT

A project manager was asked to provide support on a proposal for the U.S. Navy. This is the project managers first time working on a government proposal. The proposal manager asks the project manager to write the project management portion for the proposal. When won, the project manager will lead the project. The project manager is considering writing a lot of extras into the proposal to guarantee a win.

The proposal manager reviews the proposal answer and thought it was very good but is concerned that the response may be overstated. The project manager and the proposal manager discuss the situation. The project manager assures the proposal manager that this is normally what is done on the commercial projects. The proposal manager does not think any more about it.

The proposal is submitted to the U.S. Navy. The project manager is assigned to another project but has been promised the U.S. Navy contract, if won. It turns out that the proposal is awarded to the company. The contracting person negotiated some substantial changes to what was submitted. The project manager was not told about the changes made during contracting. The proposal work effort was made a part of the contract and again, the project manager was not told. The project manager is excited to start immediately.

1. Should the project manager have over promised in the proposal? Why or why not?
2. What are some of the steps that the project manager should do when starting on the contract?
3. What should the project and proposal managers do on future engagements?

SECTION EIGHT
TRANSPORTATION AND LOGISTICS WORKBOOK

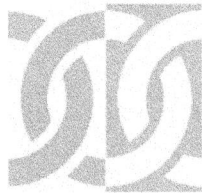

Case Study: Florida Department of Transportation: Options to Improve the I-95 Traffic Corridor

Case Study Introduction

This scenario will explore the various options available to the Florida Department of Transportation (FDOT) with regard to easing the traffic situation along the I-95 corridor from South Florida to Central Florida. Although there is a light rail system under construction (All Aboard Florida), the traffic congestion along this route is still quite high. There is a turnpike that parallels the I-95 corridor; however, there are still over 72,000 vehicles per day along this road (I-95 Corridor Coalition, n.d.). The light rail system might reduce traffic. However, there still needs to be public road improvements to connect South Florida to the rest of the nation.

Florida Department of Transportation

This case study shall explore the current situation with the Florida road system. At this time, Florida is experiencing a huge increase in road traffic spurred on by the recent reduction in fuel costs. As airlines continue to keep air rates high, more and more local consumers are driving from South Florida to all of the great attractions in Central Florida. Although there is a rail system being built to reduce traffic from South Florida to Central Florida, this option is still years away, and it is still unclear if this will even be a viable transportation option. The I-95 corridor is almost 2,000 miles of highway along the U.S. East Coast and represents 21% of the roads in the United States (I-95 Corridor Coalition, n.d.). To address the congestion issues on the I-95, the FDOT is considering four different options. First, there is the potential for a new road to parallel the I-95 in the areas that are often congested. Second, there is the potential to widen the I-95 in key areas. Third, there is the potential to add ramp metering to slow the flow of traffic and reduce congestion. Fourth, there is the potential to add more high-occupancy vehicle (HOV) lanes in critical areas.

New Road

This option considers adding a parallel road in the areas of greatest congestion along the way. A new road would mean creating an "express lane" that would avoid the congestion in Boca Raton and West Palm Beach. Given that many people transiting on the I-95 are going to Central Florida, it would be possible to create a new express lane for traffic that does not stop in these cities. A new road would offer an option for drivers and reduce the congestion in these urban areas. This option would likely be the most costly and would take the longest period to implement.

It is also likely that this additional road would become available for cars after the implementation of the rail system. The roads will be more congested and likely this will drive ridership to the rail system. However, once the alternative road becomes available, most people would return to driving as an alternative. The All Aboard Florida train project is estimated to cost $3 billion (Sigo, 2014). However, it claims private funding, but the largest holder of the debt is the U.S. government. A new road would make a state-funded road compete with a nationally funded railroad. Given that Amtrak has lost $45 billion over 44 years makes one wonder why a second road was not built rather than considering light rail (Sabas, 2015).

Road Widening

This option looks at expanding the number of lanes on the I-95 to allow more traffic to flow freely. The widening of the I-95 would improve traffic in the congested areas of Boca Raton and West Palm Beach. However, because the widening of the roads does not extend the full length of the I-95, there will likely still be congestion when the road reaches an area where there are fewer lanes. The change in the number of lanes might create new bottlenecks of traffic. This road work would also impede existing traffic for years until the work is complete. This option is less expensive than a new road, but it could help reduce traffic until the rail system comes online.

Ramp Metering

This option considers adding ramp meter that will slow the number of cars to enter the I-95 based on the amount of traffic entering the roadway. This option would add ramp meters throughout key entry points to the highway and better control the number of cars on the road. The slower cars can enter the road, the better the flow of traffic. This option has been successful in other areas and seems to be effective during peak traffic periods. It does not stop the traffic from happening, but it certainly alleviates the massive traffic congestion that happens when left unmonitored.

HOV Lane

This option is to add an HOV lane to certain areas to encourage the use of carpools. The creation of specific new HOV lanes in certain areas could ease traffic in congested areas. However, the implementation of an HOV lane would require the addition of technology to monitor carpools as well as to require additional enforcement to ensure compliance. The addition of an HOV lane has been successful in other areas and certainly has some potential. In other areas of Florida, the HOV lane is made so that others can use the HOV lane at a cost. Costs vary with traffic and can be as low as $1.00 but can go as high as $10.00 during peak times. Additional revenue from non-HOV drivers could offset some of the costs and the costs of maintenance.

Case Study Questions

1. Given these alternatives, rank these alternative(s) to make a recommended to the Florida DOT to budget for the next fiscal year?

2. What is the best alternative from a financial standpoint if the Florida DOT needed to select the least expensive option to address traffic and congestion along the I-95 corridor?

Case Study Question One Solution

To this end, the total cost of ownership needs to be considered because the state will not have a surplus of funds in the future. For this analysis, a net present value (NPV) analysis will be sufficient to show the total ownership costs. Each considered project will need to examine initial costs and consider long-term costs to determine the lowest cost acceptable solution.

Costs	New	Road	Ramp	HOV
Initial cost	25	15	5	18
Maintenance	2	1.5	0.5	1.8
Annual user	1	1	0.7	1

Figure 13: Estimated costs by project

The costs in Figure 13 were estimated to calculate the project costs for each option. All costs are in tens of millions, and each option was reviewed based on a 5% interest rate, with a payback period of 20 years. Figure 14 explains the comparison between the net present values of the various options.

Compare A to B	Compare B to C	Compare C to D
10	10	Everything in D is more
6.23	12.46	A.
0	3.74	B.
$ (3.77)	(18.72)	C.
D.	E.	F.
B is better than A	C is better than B	C is better than D

Figure 14: Cost comparisons of different options

Case Study Question Two Solution

If the FDOT budget is tight in FY2016 and beyond, the clear choice to reduce congestion on the roadway would be to implement the option of ramp metering along the I-95 corridor. Ramp metering would be the lowest cost solution to reduce the congestion along the I-95 corridor and would avoid implementing one of the higher cost solutions.

Case Study: Preserving the Wetlands or Developing the Transportation Infrastructure

Wetlands in the United States are disappearing at an alarming rate. There appears to be no form of consideration to many critical values of this nationally treasured land. Many valuable wetland areas disappear daily as a result of the development of roads, highways, railroads, and other needs of transportation. There appears to be an ignoring of the aesthetic, educational, and recreational value of this type of natural environment. The visual cultural values of wetlands remain a finite natural resource. Although people enjoy the wetlands, this area is also a preserve for so many unique species that the destruction of these areas endangers the already struggling flora and fauna (America's Everglades—The largest subtropical wilderness in the United States, n.d.). The narrow view that wetland areas are not needed is shocking, and the only way to change this behavior is to change our destructive habits in these limited regions.

The Clash of Progress and Preservation

Preserving wetlands and supporting progress continues to be a significant challenge for transportation developers. Preserving wetlands should not become a separate task from preserving the natural landscape of the region. The national parks are currently celebrating a centennial of preservation. Therefore, there must be continued effort to preserve these education centers that are also natural recreation areas (Wang, 2011). It is hard to imagine a nation without national parks, however, since the park service has only existed for 100 years and our nation is over 200 years old, there clearly was a time when the environment was secondary to progress. Our ancestors clearly had a vision; the preservation of this vision should be a social requirement. Anything less would mean that our generation fails as stewards of the land.

Concerning the cultural area, all ecosystems must be preserved. Civilization must preserve the cultural values handed down by the previous generations. The management of these cultural issues must address the environment in a manner that promotes and enhances the natural beauty of the area. Otherwise, our nation becomes a victim of its success and then it allows technology and progress to trump the natural beauty. A society that allows that will freely pollute and destroy their natural resources, until they run out. For those that disagree, a quick trip to China should set the record straight because the pollution has become so bad there that international athletes refused to compete outside. Therefore, everyone must become a steward of the environment and must do their part to ensure the success of the roles that are played by these features are well enhanced (Rushton, Croucher, & Baker, 2010).

Case Study Questions

1. Should any transportation network be considered in wetland areas?
2. Light rail has been shown to be less obtrusive to the enviroment, should light rail be considered instead of a highway?

SECTION NINE
REVERSE LOGISTICS WORKBOOK

CASE STUDY: IMPLEMENTING WORRY FREE RETURNS

Organizations must recognize that all retail companies, especially electronics companies, are competing for the same consumer market. In the past, local retail operators competed with other local retails for market share in a specific geographic location. Local electronics companies must not only compete with other local companies, but they must compete with e-retailers and other less-than-local competition that have competition leveling services such as free shipping or other discounts targeted at out of area consumers. If this were not enough, operations managers have to cope with larger and more complex organizations making it harder for managers to be available to address new issues. Organizations are moving to be more specialized and more streamlined in their focus.

Retail electronics companies are removing returns from their supply chain and having consumers return material directly to the manufacturer. Rather than managing these returns through their supply chain, they are having consumers deal with another company. Many retail outlets, online and face-to-face, have a disclaimer not to return the product to the store where it was initially purchased. Instead, retail stores have consumers mail the defective good via some UPS drop or other organization whose name does not resemble that original store or product manufacturer.

Most organizations accept that a very small portion of distributed goods will be returned for some other reason. In many cases, the reason for the return is unclear, and many organizations simply ignore the returns as long as the returns are not quality related or highly visible to the media. The reason that this important information is ignored is that there is no one to own the problem. For example, quality circles tend to manufacture quality; procurement professionals attend to sub-contractor and supplier quality, and so there is no one left to attend to the quality outside of these important areas.

Reverse Logistics and Returns

Studies in reverse logistics have shown that there is always a portion of products that are returned and tested, but the company fails to identify any issue with the product. These "no fault returns" cost the company money in time and prestige. Interestingly, these "no fault returns" will often outnumber the quantity that is returned for actual quality issues, yet few organizations try to learn what the cause of these types of returns is. Many remain focused on reducing manufacturing errors and remain ignorant to the real problem with their returns.

Another important matter to consider is the actual costs associated with reverse logistics. The reported value of U.S. returns alone is estimated at 100 billion per year and consists of ~4% of the U.S. GDP (Li & Olorunniwo, 2008; Stock & Mulki, 2009). This information shows the importance of the management of returns, not even considering the other areas associated with reverse logistics. Further studies have shown that the rate of returns can vary between 5% and 50% (Rogers & Tibben-Lembke, 1998) and so even at a modest 5% rate, this level of returns is significant.

Assuming that 5% of a company's value is tied up in reverse logistics can have serious brand ramifications, this alone should be sufficient for an organization to address this significant issue. Given the erosion of margins in most market segments given the current state of the economy, 5% can be the difference between success and failure. Even considering a highly efficient organization might have scant 0.5% returns (1 in 200), this is significantly >0.00034% (3.4 per million) that Six Sigma promised to deliver. Clearly, there is more at work than just quality with regard to returns, and hence organizations must take notice of this situation and apply management solutions to achieve a clear competitive advantage.

Worry Free Returns

Given all this background regarding reverse logistics Diamond Electronics, a local but well regarded retail electronics store is considering implementing a policy of "worry free returns" where a customer can return any item within 30 days of purchase. Diamond Electronics feels that this could offer a competitive advantage to the organization over the online retailers and Big Box stores that have been cutting into their business. However, Diamond Electronics is not sure how to implement this new organizational initiative. Diamond Electronics has a very professional supply chain with skilled negotiators and professional managers to control the flow of materials for the organization. This professionalism has been shown to support quality assurance, risk management, and operations. Diamond Electronics understand that having a highly trained and professional supply chain group will yield organizational benefits beyond the cost of these professionals. The problem is that Diamond Electronics is not sure if they should give this new initiative to the supply chain group, or if they should create a new group that should be responsible for these worry free returns.

Case Study Questions

1. Given the alternative of giving the worry free returns initiative to the supply chain group or creating a new group, which alternative would offer the best results? Why?

2. What is the best alternative from a financial standpoint is the least expensive option to address the worry free returns institutive? Why?

CASE STUDY: USING A THIRD PARTY TO HANDLE REVERSE LOGISTICS

Many organizations have decided that rather develop their own internal reverse logistics expertise, they should instead outsource the function. There are advantages to outsourcing the function to a separate organization that is a specialist in the field. Utilizing a third party allows the organization to benefit from the external organization's economies of scale and their subject matter experts.

One economic benefit is transaction consolidation. Transactional consolidation is the method of accumulating transactions of firms with smaller volumes to create one firm with a large number of transactions. This allows the company to concentrate purchases with fewer vendors. It would also allow for consolidation of transactions and allow flexibility, such as monthly billing rather than on an order by order basis. Outsourcing would increase efficiencies by reducing the paper flow within an organization. This type of efficiency will create labor-saving systems that will improve the process flow.

Case Study Questions

1. Describe the positives associated with using a third party to handle reverse logistics for a company.

2. Describe the negatives associated with using a third party to handle reverse logistics for a company.

REFERENCES

Amazon. (n.d.). *Amazon*. Retrieved from Amazon: http://www.amazon.com.

American Bureau of Shipping. (n.d.). Rule requirements for materials and welding. Retrieved from Eagle.org: https://www.eagle.org/eagleExternalPortalWEB/ShowProperty/BEA%20Repository/Rules&Guides/Archives/2_SteelVesselRules2000/Part2MaterialsWelding.

America's Everglades—The largest subtropical wilderness in the United States. (n.d.). Retrieved April 7, 2016, from Everglades National Park Florida: https://www.nps.gov/ever/index.htm.

Apple. (n.d.). *Apple Returns policy*. Retrieved from Apple: http://store.apple.com/us/help/returns_refund.

Araujo, F. (2016, June 19). *Chinese company beats Amazon to deliver online goods by unmanned drone*. Retrieved from Mirror: http://www.mirror.co.uk/news/world-news/chinese-company-beats-amazon-deliver-8230920.

Associated Press. (2014, July 12). *Amazon asks FAA for permission to test its delivery drones*. Retrieved from Fox News: http://www.foxnews.com/tech/2014/07/12/amazon-asks-faa-for-permission-to-use-drones-to-deliver-packages/.

Atiyeh, C., & Blackwell, R. (2016, March 2). *Massive Takata airbag recall: Everything you need to know, including full list of affected vehicles*. Retrieved from Car and Driver: http://blog.caranddriver.com/massive-takata-airbag-recall-everything-you-need-to-know-including-full-list-of-affected-vehicles/.

Backlund, F., Chronéer, D., & Sundqvist, E. (2015). Maturity assessment: Towards continuous improvements for project-based organisations. *International Journal of Managing Projects in Business*, *8*(2), 256–278. doi:10.1108/IJMPB-05-2014-0047

Beauchamp, T. L., & Bowie, N. E. (1997) *Ethical theory and business (5ᵗʰ ed.)* Englewood Cliffs, NJ: Prentice-Hall.

Bishop, L. (2016, February 1). *Best Buy's recycling program is changing. Here's how and why.* Retrieved from Best Buy Corporate: https://corporate.bestbuy.com/10556-2/.

Blanchard, D. (2010). *Supply chain management: Best practices.* Hoboken, NJ: Wiley.

Blanchard, D. (2012, February). Going in Reverse Can Be the Right Direction: Returns management can offer significant cost savings for manufacturers. Industry Week. [Electronic Version]. Available at http://www.industryweek.com/articles/going_in_ reverse_can_be_the_right_direction_26594.aspx?SectionID=2.

Boyer, K. K., & Verma, R. (2010). *Operations & supply chain managment for the 21st century.* Mason, OH: Cengage Learning.

Cârstea, C. (2014). IT project management—cost, time and quality. *Economy Transdisciplinarity Cognition, 17*(1), 28.

Clark, C. (2015, October 19). *Rio Tinto using self driving trucks to transport ore.* Retrieved from Business Insider: http://www.businessinsider.com/rio-tinto-using-self-driving-trucks-to-transport-ore-2015-10?r=UK&IR=T.

Creswell, J. (2003). *Research design: Qualitative, quantitative, and mixed methods approaches.* Thousand Oaks, CA: Sage Publications, Inc.

Curlee, W., & Gordon, R. (2010). *Complexity theory and project management.* Hoboken, NJ: Wiley.

Curtis, S. (2016, May 25). *Pizza Hut hires ROBOT waiters to take orders and process payments at its fast-food restaurants.* Retrieved from Mirror: http://www.mirror.co.uk/tech/pizza-hut-hires-robot-waiters-8045172.

Davies, A. (2013, April 12). *11 ways airlines are cramming people on to planes and saving money.* Retrieved from Business Insider: http://www.businessinsider.com/ways-airlines-are-cutting-weight-2013-4.

Davies, A. (2014, October 7). *Mercedes is making a self-driving semi to change the future of shipping.* Retrieved from Wired: https://www.wired.com/2014/10/mercedes-making-self-driving-semi-change-future-shipping/.

Dockrill, P. (2016). *This 5,000-year-old artefact shows ancient workers were paid in beer.*

Retrieved from Science Alters: http://www.sciencealert.com/this-5-000-year-old-clay-tablet-shows-ancient-mesopotamians-were-paid-for-work-in-beer.

Duarte, D., & Snyder, N. (2006). *Mastering virtual teams* (3rd ed.). San Francisco, CA: Jossey-Bass.

Fernholz, T. (2013, March 12). *The US drone economy will create 100,000 jobs, say companies who make drones*. Retrieved from Quartz: http://qz.com/61727/the-us-drone-economy-will-create-100000-jobs-say-companies-who-make-drones/.

Fernie, J., & Sparks, L. (2014). *Logistics and retail management: Emerging issues and new challenges in the retail supply chain*. Philidelphia, PA: Kogan Page.

Franzen, C. (2016, April 1). *Elon musk says nearly 200,000 tesla model 3 cars pre-ordered in 24 hours*. Retrieved from Popular Science: http://www.popsci.com/elon-musk-says-180000-tesla-model-3-cars-pre-ordered-in-24-hours.

Frej, W. (2016, May 2). *It's now illegal for supermarkets to waste food in France*. Retrieved from The World Post: http://www.huffingtonpost.com/entry/france-supermarkets-food-waste_us_56b4ba4de4b04f9b57d93f53.

Garrett, G. (2010). *World class contracting* (5th ed). Chicago, IL: Wolters Kluwer Law & Business.

Gaudin, S. (2015, March 12). *Hotel guests open the door to a robotic butler*. Retrieved from Computer World: http://www.computerworld.com/article/2895791/hotel-guests-open-the-door-to-a-robotic-butler.html.

Gordon, R. (2011). *Reverse logistics management*. Hoboken, NJ: Wiley.

Gordon, R., & Curlee, W. (2011). *The virtual project management office: Best practices, proven methods*. Vienna, VA: Management Concepts.

GSA. (2015, July 17). *Recycling Program*. Retrieved from GSA Environmental Programs: www.gsa.gov/recyclingprogram.

Gustafsson, M., Smyth, H., Ganskau, E., & Arhippainen, T. (2010). Bridging strategic and operational issues for project business through managing trust. *International Journal of Managing Projects in Business, 3*(3), 422–442. doi: http://dx.doi.org/10.1108/17538371011056066

Haan, H. J. (2014). More insight from physics into the construction of the Egyptian pyramids. *Archaeometry, 56*(1), 145–174. doi: 10.1111/j.1475-4754.2012.00726.x

Hapag-Lloyd. (n.d.). *Container ships soon to sail unmanned?* Retrieved from Hapag-Lloyd: https://www.hapag-lloyd.com/en/press_and_media/insight_page_42532.html.

Hazen, J. K., & Lynch, C. F. (2008). *The role of transportation in the supply chain.* Memphis, TN: CFL Publishing.

Hedgepeth, O., Henrie, M., & Hedgepeth Jr., O. (n.d.). *RFID Is the Alaska Gas Pipeline's Strongest Link.* Retrieved from RFID Journal: http://www.rfidjournal.com/articles/view?2670/3.

Hoffman, W. (2006, March). Shifting into reverse: As supply chains grow more complex, shippers realize need for a separate returns process for speed, cost savings. *Traffic World,* p. 19, Commonwealth Business media.

Inbound Logistics. (2013, December). *Panama Canal Expansion: Changing the Channel.* Retrieved from Inbound Logistics: http://www.inboundlogistics.com/cms/article/panama-canal-expansion-changing-the-channel/.

Jacobs, R. F., Berry, W., Whybark, D., & Vollman, T. (2011). *Manufacturing planning and control for supply chain management* (6th ed.). New York: McGraw-Hill.

Kerzner, H. R. (2014). *Project management 2.0.* Hoboken, NJ: Wiley.

Knapp, G. (2015). The Incas, (2nd ed). *Journal of Latin American Geography, 14*(2), 205.

Korhonen, T., Laine, T., & Martinsuo, M. (2014). Management control of project portfolio uncertainty: A managerial role perspective. *Project Management Journal, 45*(1), 21–37. doi: 10.1002/pmj.21390

Kornfeld, B. J., & Kara, S. (2011). Project portfolio selection in continuous improvement. *International Journal of Operations & Production Management, 31*(10), 1071–1088. doi: http://dx.doi.org/10.1108/01443571111172435.

Kwak, Y. H., & Anbari, F. T. (2012). History, practices, and future of earned value management in government: Perspectives from NASA. *Project Management Journal, 43*(1), 77–90. doi: 10.1002/pmj.20272

LaMonica, P. (2016, May 23). *This self-driving car company is on fire*. Retrieved from CNN Money: http://money.cnn.com/2016/05/23/investing/self-driving-car-nvidia/.

Larter, D. (2016, April 10). *Meet the Navy's new sub-hunting drone ship*. Retrieved from NavyTimes: http://www.navytimes.com/story/military/2016/04/08/meet-navys-new-sub-hunting-drone-ship/82798450/.

Lerch, M., & Spieth, P. (2013). Innovation project portfolio management: A qualitative analysis. *IEEE Transactions on Engineering Management, 60*(1), 18–29. doi:10.1109/TEM.2012.2201723

Levin, G. (2010). *Interpersonal skills for portfolio, program, and project managers*. Vienna, VA.: Management Concepts.

Levin, G. & Wyzalek, J. (Eds.). (2015). *Portfolio management: A strategic approach*. Boca Raton, FL.: CRC Press.

Li, X., & Olorunniwo, F. (2008). An exploration of reverse logistics practices in three companies. *Supply Chain Management: An International Journal, 13*(5), 381–386. Emerald Group Publishing

Lin, Y. R. (2015). Project portfolio management for social responsibility reporting. *Global Conference on Business & Finance Proceedings, 10*(2), 127.

Lippert, J. (2016, April 25). *On this waterfront, robot longshoremen are the new contenders*. Retrieved from Bloomberg Technology: http://www.bloomberg.com/news/articles/2016-04-25/on-this-waterfront-robot-longshoremen-are-the-new-contenders.

MacLennan, A. (2013). *4 Interesting airline cost-cutting approaches*. Retrieved March 24, 2016, from http://www.fool.com/investing/general/2013/10/30/4-interesting-airline-cost-cutting-approaches.aspx.

Malik, M.A. Khalfan, McDermott, P., & Swan, W. (2007). Building trust in construction projects. *Supply Chain Management, 12*(6), 385–391. doi: http://dx.doi.org/10.1108/13598540710826308

MAREX. (2014, October 5). *U.S. Navy Tests Autonomous Swarm Boats*. Retrieved from Maritime Executive: http://www.maritime-executive.com/article/US-Navy-Tests-

Autonomous-Swarm-Boats-2014-10-05.

Mathews, L. (2015, April 21). *U.S. Postal Service selects drone as potential new delivery vehicle.* Retrieved from Geek: http://www.geek.com/news/u-s-postal-service-selects-drone-as-potential-new-delivery-vehicle-1620904/

Müller, R., Martinsuo, M., & Blomquist, T. (2008). Project portfolio control and portfolio management performance in different contexts. *Project Management Journal, 39*(3), 28–42. doi: 10.1002/pmj.20053

Näsholm, M. H., & Blomquist, T. (2015). Co-creation as a strategy for program management. *International Journal of Managing Projects in Business, 8*(1), 58–73. doi: 10.1108/IJMPB-10-2013-0063

NCMA. (2013). *Contract management body of knowledge (CMBOK)* (4th ed.). National Contract Management Association: Ashburn, VA. ISBN-13:978-0-9700897-7-9

Nield, D. (2015, April 15). *UK company wants to deliver parcels through an automated underground tunnel system.* Retrieved from Giz Mag: http://www.gizmag.com/mole-solutions-underground-deliveries/37009/.

Nogrady, B. (2010, May 4). *We are entering the sixth wave of innovation.* Retrieved from ABC - Environment: http://www.abc.net.au/environment/articles/2010/05/04/2889772.htm.

Office of the United States Trade Representative: Executive Office of the President. (2014, May 1). *US - Mexico Trade Facts.* Retrieved from Office of the United States Trade Representative: Executive Office of the President: https://ustr.gov/countries-regions/americas/mexico.

Office of the United States Trade Representative: Executive Office of the President. (n.d.a). *US Canada trade facts.* Retrieved from Office of the United States Trade Representative: Executive Office of the President: https://ustr.gov/countries-regions/americas/canada.

Office of the United States Trade Representative: Executive Office of the President. (n.d.b). *Bilateral agreements.* Retrieved from Office of the United States Trade Representative: Executive Office of the President: https://ustr.gov/countries-regions/americas/mexico/bilateral-agreements.

Pheng, L., & Lee, B. (1997). 'Managerial grid' and Zhuge Liang's 'Art of management': Integration of effective project management. *Management Decision, 35*(5/6), 382.

PotGuide Colorado. (n.d.). *Marijuana laws in Colorado.* Retrieved from PotGuide.com: https://www.coloradopotguide.com/marijuana-laws-in-colorado/.

Project Management Institute. (2008). *A guide to project management book of knowledge.* (PMOK® Guide) (4th ed.). Newton Square, PA: Project Management Institute.

Project Management Institute (Ed.). (2013a). *A guide to the project management body of knowledge* (5th ed.). Sylva, NC: PMI Publishing Division.

Project Management Institute (Ed.). (2013b). *The standard for program management* (3rd ed.). Sylva, NC: PMI Publishing Division.

Project Management Institute (Ed.). (2013c). *The standard for portfolio management* (3rd ed.). Sylva, NC: PMI Publishing Division.

Project Management Institute Thought Leadership Series Report (Ed.). (2015a). *Implementing the project portfolio: A vital C-suite focus.* Newtown Square, PA: PMI.

Project Management Institute Thought Leadership Series Report (Ed.). (2015b). *Delivering on strategy: The power of project portfolio management.* Newtown Square, PA: PMI.

Rauwald, C., & Tschampa, D. (2014, September 18). *Mercedes-Benz to Test Self-Driving Cars on California Roads.* Retrieved from Bloomberg Technologies: http://www.bloomberg.com/news/articles/2014-09-18/mercedes-benz-to-test-self-driving-cars-on-california-roads.

Republic of Panama. (2015, February). *Panama Canal Expansion.* Retrieved from Official Website of the Panama Canal Expansion: http://micanaldepanama.com/expansion/.

Rogers, D., & Tibbens-Lembke, R. (1998). *Going backwards: Reverse logistics trends and practices.* Reverse Logistics Executive Council. [Electronic Version] Retrieved on January 19, 2012 from http://www.rlec.org/reverse.pdf.

Rushton, A., Croucher, P., & Baker, P. (2010). *The handbook of logistics & distribution management.* London: Kogan Page.

Sabas, M. (2015, March 6). *Amtrack bill continues history wasted subsidies.* Retrieved from E21: http://www.economics21.org/html/amtrak-bill-continues-history-wasted-subsidies-1263.html.

Schlangenstein, M., & Sasso, M. (2016, January 27). *The cost of airline fuel drops will airline prices stay steady.* Retrieved from Skift: https://skift.com/2016/01/27/the-cost-of-airline-fuel-drops-while-airplane-ticket-prices-stay-steady/.

Schreffler, M. J. (2014). Inca architecture from the Andes to the Adriatic: Pedro Sancho's description of Cuzco. *Renaissance Quarterly, 67*(4), 1191–1223. doi: 10.1086/679781

Schwalbe, K. (2011). *Information Technology Project Management* (6th ed.), CENGAGE Learning.

Scott, M. (2011, July 20). *Airlines look to fuel savings techniques as EU ETS draws closer.* Retrieved from Flightglobal Aviation Connected: https://www.flightglobal.com/news/articles/airlines-look-to-fuel-saving-techniques-as-eu-ets-draws-359650/.

Sigo, S. (2014, September 17). *The Bond Buyer.* Retrieved from Private Passenger Rail Service Plan in Florida Questioned: http://www.bondbuyer.com/news/regionalnews/private-passenger-rail-service-plan-in-florida-questioned-1066237-1.html

Slack, N., Chambers, S., & Johnson, R. (2010). *Operations management* (6th ed.). Essex, England: Prentice Hall.

Stock, J. (2001, March 1). The 7 deadly sins of reverse logistics. Retrieved from Material Handling & Logistics: http://mhlnews.com/facilities-management/7-deadly-sins-reverse-logistics.

Stock, J., & Mulki, J. (2009). Product returns processing: An examination of practices of manufacturers, wholesalers/distributors and retailers. *Journal of Business Logistics, 30*(1), 33–62. ABI/INFORM Global.

Stringer, L. (2009). *The green workplace: Sustainable strategies that benefit employees, the environment, and the bottom line.* New York, NY: Palgrave Macmillan. ISBN: 978-0-230-61428-4.

Tablyn, T. (2016, February 23). *Delivery drone company to start testing robots on London streets next month*. Retrieved from Huffington Post: http://www.huffingtonpost.co.uk/2016/02/23/delivery-drone-company-to-start-testing-robots-on-london-streets-next-month_n_9296594.html.

Turban, E., King, D., Lee, J., Liang, T.-P., & Turban, D. (2012). *Electronic commerce 2012: Managerial and social networks perspective*. New York: Pearson.

US Government. (2015, November 3). *Safecar.gov*. Retrieved from Recalls Spotlight: Takata Air Bag Recalls: http://www.safercar.gov/rs/takata/takata-presscon110315.html.

Volpicelli, G. (2016, March 18). *Domino's is trialing an autonomous pizza delivery robot*. Retrieved from ARS Technica: http://arstechnica.com/gadgets/2016/03/dominos-pizza-delivery-robot/.

Walmart. (2014, February 19). *Introducing the Walmart Advanced Vehicle Experience concept truck*. Retrieved from YouTube: https://youtu.be/iTTgxqZqTaA.

Wang, G. (2011). Supply chain integration based on commerce flow and logistics. *Contemporary Logistics*, 91–97. http://dx.doi.org/10.5503/j.cl.2011.02.015.

Wisner, J., Tan, K.-C., & Leong, G. K. (2012). *Principles of supply chain management: A balanced approach*. Mason, OH: South-Western Cengage Learning.

Wong, Z. (2007). *Human factors in project management*. San Francisco, CA: Jossey-Bass. ISBN: 978-0-7879-9629-1

www.ingramcontent.com/pod-product-compliance
Lightning Source LLC
Chambersburg PA
CBHW051335200326
41519CB00026B/7438